CARRINGTON

Christopher Hampton was born in the Azores in 1946. He wrote his first play, *When Did You Last See My Mother?* at the age of eighteen. His work for the theatre, television and cinema includes the *Philanthropist*, adaptations of Ibsen and Molière, and the screenplay *Dangerous Liaisons. Carrington*, which marks his directorial début, opened at Cannes in 1995 to critical acclaim.

CARRINGTON
Christopher Hampton

faber and faber
LONDON · BOSTON

First published in 1995 by Faber and Faber Limited
3 Queen Square London WCIN 3AU

Photoset by Parker Typesetting Service, Leicester
Printed in England by Clays Ltd, St Ives plc

A CIP record of this book
is available from the British Library
ISBN 0-571-15336-4

2 4 6 8 10 9 7 5 3

The white elephant

The gestation period of *Carrington* (more or less eighteen years) was so grossly excessive and its halting progress so convoluted and strewn with landmines, it seemed worth attempting an account, especially in view of the fact that its entirely unexpected conclusion has brought about a radical alteration in my life.

As far as I recall, it was Barry Krost, then a London-based agent, who in the mid-seventies gave me Michael Holroyd's monumental and ground-breaking biography of Lytton Strachey. He was convinced there was some sort of film to be derived from it and had already suggested this to his friend and future client John Osborne, who had sensibly declined, although he was sufficiently impressed by the strange story of Lytton and Carrington to use elements of it in his underrated play of that year *Watch It Come Down*. I was less prudent: I was so shaken and haunted by Holroyd's devastating book that I told Barry if he could find some credible source of finance for what was obviously an unconventional subject, I'd be more than happy to take it on, even though I had no clear idea how I might extrapolate from this mass of material some manageable narrative.

A year or so later, I was working with Stephen Frears, rehearsing my first original play for television, when Barry called to say that an executive from Warner Bros. was in London and was expressing some interest in commissioning a script which might in some way encompass the nebulous but then fashionable subject of Bloomsbury. Could I lunch with him? I should add that the mid-seventies sprouted one of the very occasional oases in the featureless desert which is the British film industry of the last thirty years. These brief periods of relief always baffled and angered the government of the day, which would eventually devise some countermeasure, the closure, say, of some harmless tax loophole or the threatened penalization of potential foreign investors or even some entirely illogical and unhelpful strengthening of the currency. Anything, in short, to put a stop to the embarrassing prospect of producing in any given year more than the usual dribble of Poverty Row features. In 1976, then, someone at the Department of Trade and Industry had nodded; the dollar was strong, and things British became fleetingly attractive to the Hollywood studios.

A car came to collect me from the Acton Hilton (the BBC rehearsal rooms) and whisked me into the West End. According to the piece of paper someone had handed me, I was to lunch with a Mr Elephant, which seemed, like most things I associated with Hollywood, unlikely but not impossible. Mr Elephant greeted me warmly, a man more bearish than owlish, and, in traditional fashion, chatted affably of this and that, not uttering the word 'Bloomsbury' until the arrival of coffee, and even then with an apologetic intonation. I admitted that I had little or no interest in Bloomsbury as such, but that I was touched and fascinated by the story of Carrington, which I proceeded to relate to him. He listened in a thoughtful and sympathetic manner and pronounced himself very interested; I explained I had to get back to my rehearsals and thanked him for an excellent lunch, addressing him as 'Mr Elephant', which he gave every appearance of taking on the chin. Only as the car pulled away and I looked back at the restaurant did it seem likely that some clerical error had occurred: we'd been lunching at The White Elephant.

Nevertheless and somewhat to my amazement, a contract very soon arrived and I retired to my house in Oxfordshire, a Georgian rectory within walking distance of the spot where Carrington began her campaign to seduce Gerald Brenan in 1921, and settled down for what was very probably the most enjoyable year of my writing life. It was the first time I'd worked for one of the big studios and I found them endlessly accommodating. No sooner did you make an enquiry about the entire Lytton–Carrington correspondence stored on microfiche in the British Museum than a truck would arrive with cartons and cartons of photocopies. After the tropical rigours of 1976, the summer of '77 was the full buzzing and humming genuine British article (very similar, in fact, to the summer of 1994, when the film was eventually shot), and I strung a hammock between the trees at the top of the garden (there was a new baby in the house) and immersed myself in another world. Six months of planning gave way to three months' writing through the height of the summer and a first draft completed by the middle of September. I knew it was about twice as long as it should be, but I was pleased with the script and confident that a good director would know where to apply the machete.

I imagine the delivery of the *Carrington* script must have caused some consternation at Warner Bros. Certainly Mr Elephant (whose real name turned out to be Marty Elfand, so not too much of a clerical error) had long since been released and whoever inherited the project must have been more than a little bewildered. Nevertheless, they buckled down to it and within four or five months I was asked if I could go over to Los Angeles and spend a couple of weeks working with the designated director, Herbert Ross. By all means, I said, provided they were able to cope with the fact that I couldn't drive.

It turned out that the only hotel within walking distance of Herb Ross's house was one of the most expensive in Beverly Hills. Indeed, the suite they installed me in was so extensive I couldn't at first find the bed and it was only when I was settling down on the sofa that I finally spotted the discreet staircase which led up to the three bedrooms above. Mr Ross had a play in preview and a film in pre-production, both by his usual collaborator, Neil Simon, so he was a little distracted, but I was happy to get back to the hotel in time for the daily distribution of free caviar at 6 p.m. in the Roof Bar, and our script discussions were extremely straightforward and constructive. Finally, on the last day, Barry Krost hosted a lunch in a private room at Mr Chow's. I was sitting between Herb Ross and his wife, the late Nora Kaye, a formidable and celebrated ex-ballet dancer and principal of the American Ballet Theater. The two of them were soon engaged in a ferocious argument about China: during a frosty silence I turned to Nora and, thinking a change of subject might be helpful, asked her if she had read the script. 'I read some of it,' she said.

Her tone was unambiguous, but for some reason I persisted and asked her what she thought of it. She told me she didn't like it. How much of it had she read? I asked. Nine pages, she admitted. Perhaps, I suggested, it wasn't fair to judge it quite so definitively on so short an extract and she should give it another chance. She looked straight at me. 'I don't want to read about a lot of pissy English people,' she remarked.

I looked at Barry Krost: he had gone white. At this point, the door burst open and a girl in hot pants erupted into the room. She was carrying a cake which said *Carrington* in pink icing. The next day I flew back to London and never heard another word.

1980 was Lytton Strachey's centenary and the *South Bank Show* asked Michael Holroyd to write a programme about him. In the course of our mutual vicissitudes, Michael and I had become friends and he suggested that extracts from my script might be used to illustrate the programme. Warner Bros. kindly consented to a maximum of eight minutes from the script being used, and so it was that Joanna David, Edward Petherbridge and the late Geoffrey Burridge were the first to incarnate scenes from the script. The programme was well received, won a prize in America and was seen by my friend Peter Gill, who, three or four years later, asked if he could use the script for actors' exercises in the National Theatre Studio, which he ran at that time.

Sometime in 1984, Peter rang me to say that he had decided to give a staged reading of *Carrington* as one of his studio nights at the Cottesloe. It was done with a couple of dozen actors (some reading the stage directions) sitting on plain chairs on the Cottesloe stage. The theatre was full and the occasion was, for me, a full seven years after completing the script, extremely moving. And the following day I had two enquiries from television companies. One of these was from Linda Agran at Thames TV who, with enormous determination, eventually persuaded the company to buy back the rights from Warner Bros. at a mere seven times my original salary (perhaps the caviar had not, after all, been free). No sooner had this transaction been completed than Linda, following some pattern I had begun to recognize as inevitable, lost her job. Her successor, however, an ebullient New Zealander called Andrew

Brown, liked the script very much, as did his colleague John Hambley, the head of Thames TV's film division, Euston. There seemed no reason on earth why the film should not now smoothly proceed to production.

On the plus side we also had the enthusiastic support of Jeremy Isaacs and David Rose at Channel 4; Andrew Brown brought in Mike Newell, for whom I had already written a screenplay from Peter Prince's novel *The Good Father*; and we had made contact with two French companies which were extremely interested in the project: Pyramide, run by Francis Boespflug and Fabienne Vonier and Noréa, which was Phillipe Carcassonne's shingle. But every positive was to be undone by some over-achieving negative. The powers-that-were at Thames had some deep objection to the script (its cost perhaps), which caused them to declare that, while they had no fundamental objection to the film being made, they were certainly not going to put any money into it themselves; hardly a confidence-inspiring posture in the eyes of potential investors. Then David Rose's successor at Channel 4, David Aukin, finally admitted his blanket aversion to so-called 'period drama'; Andrew Brown convinced himself, when the money was finally all in place, that Mike, who was editing *The Enchanted April*, would not have sufficient time for pre-production and unilaterally appointed another director, which caused the French investors to withdraw at once; and finally, to put the old tin lid on it, Thames lost its franchise.

I have an office in Notting Hill Gate where friends occasionally come and stay: one such is Ronnie Shedlo, who had bought the film rights of my first play in the mid-sixties and has been a friend ever since. Rooting around during a bout of insomnia, he found a script of *Carrington*, with which he proceeded to fall in love. He and his English partner, John McGrath, also an old friend, took up the cause and began painstakingly to try to reglue what had so comprehensively fallen part. Needless to say, they initially encountered the established pattern of setbacks and rejections, but within a mere eighteen months came a couple of decisive strokes of luck: Emma Thompson, who had given a memorably good screen test back in the days when she was only just known, agreed at once, when reapproached, to play Carrington; and Polygram, who had taken a share in Phillipe Carcassonne's company, suddenly agreed to put up all the necessary finance to make the film.

It seemed scarcely believable: only sixteen years after the delivery of the script, and here it was, set to go forward. Mike cast Jonathan Pryce and a date was agreed for the summer of 1994 when both actors were available. At which point, I received a phone call from Mike. He was dispirited about the prospects of the film he was then editing. 'It's just a little English film,' he said. 'It won't *do* anything. I can't go straight into another little English film. I have to go to Hollywood and make a proper movie.' He was unpersuadable, adamantine. The film he was working on was called *Four Weddings and a Funeral*.

All kinds of directors were frantically canvassed. They were all unavailable, uninterested or unfinanceable. And eventually, late one evening, Philippe Carcassonne called to say that in France it was not unprecedented for the writer to direct his script. 'Oh, no,' I said. 'I've never wanted to do that.' And I hadn't. But on the other hand, if I let the opportunity slip, who was to say it wouldn't be another decade or two before the actors, the dates and the money were there? So that when Emma rang a couple of days later and made the same suggestion, I was already weakening. And then, the strangest thing: like a virgin in a pornographic novel, having resisted so staunchly for so long, I found I couldn't get enough of it. And Carrington, who specialized in changing men's lives, had now changed mine.

Carrington has passed, over the years, through a minimum of eight or nine drafts, reducing, in the process, to not much more than half its original length. The final cuts were made, painfully, after the completion of the film. It seemed right, however, to print here a text as close to the finished film as might be; and this is what will be found in the following pages.

Any first-time director has a great many people to thank and I would like to express my wholehearted gratitude to every one of the cast and crew who worked on the film and helped to make

it such a magical experience. I should also like to thank
Margaret Camplejohn and Kate Rhodes James for their help in
preparing this text; all those, many mentioned above, some not,
who made their contributions over the years; my legendary
agent, the late Peggy Ramsay, who never doubted the film
would one day be made (though the notion of my directing it
would very probably have appalled her); Michael Holroyd, for
raising the subject in the first place and for his unfailing
encouragement, good-humoured resignation and friendship as
one setback seamlessly blended into another; and my wife
Laura and daughters Alice and Mary, the majority of whom
were scarcely born when I started work on *Carrington*, for their
constant support and tolerance for my preposterous profession.

Christopher Hampton, 1995

Carrington was first shown at the 1995 Cannes Film Festival.
The cast and crew includes:

CARRINGTON	Emma Thompson
LYTTON STRACHEY	Jonathan Pryce
RALPH PARTRIDGE	Steven Waddington
GERALD BRENAN	Samuel West
MARK GERTLER	Rufus Sewell
LADY OTTOLINE MORRELL	Penelope Wilton
VANESSA BELL	Janet McTeer
PHILIP MORRELL	Peter Blythe
BEACUS PENROSE	Jeremy Northam
FRANCES PARTRIDGE	Alex Kingston
ROGER SENHOUSE	Sebastian Harcombe
CLIVE BELL	Richard Clifford
MAYOR	David Ryall
MILITARY REPRESENTATIVE	Stephen Boxer
MARY HUTCHINSON	Annabel Mullion
DUNCAN GRANT	Gary Turner
MARJORIE GERTLER	Georgiana Dacombe
NURSE	Helen Blatch
COURT USHER	Neville Phillips
DR STARKEY SMITH	Christopher Birch
PORTER	Daniel Betts
FLY DRIVER	Simon Bye
GONDOLIER	Marzio Idoni
Written and directed by	Christopher Hampton
Producer	Ronald Shedlo and John McGrath
Co-producer	Chris Thompson
Editor	George Akers
Director of Photography	Denis Lenoir
Executive Producers	Francis Boespflug
	Phillipe Carcassonne
	Fabienne Vonier
Production Designer	Caroline Amies
Casting by	Fothergill & Lunn Casting
Music by	Michael Nyman
Costumer Designer	Penny Rose

For Laura

CAPTION ON BLACK SCREEN

ONE
LYTTON & CARRINGTON 1915

EXT. LEWES STATION. DAY
The hiss and clatter of a steam train.

A small, dirty engine pulls its train into the deserted station, shabby from wartime neglect. One door opens and a man steps down on to the platform and deposits his luggage. The steam clears to reveal a bizarre and astonishing figure: LYTTON STRACHEY. *He's immensely tall and thin, his limbs unnaturally elongated and his face concealed behind a luxuriant reddish beard and steel-rimmed spectacles. He is wearing an elderly, shapeless tweed suit under a cloak, a Homburg hat and a very long tartan scarf, wound several times around his neck, the ends reaching his knees. It's 1915 and he is thirty-five.*

He leaves the train door open and makes no attempt to advance down the platform: simply waiting by his suitcase until a very young PORTER *appears through the steam.* LYTTON *brightens perceptibly.*

The PORTER *rushes towards* LYTTON *and picks up his case.*

LYTTON: Hello . . .
PORTER: Sir . . .
  (*The* PORTER *leads* LYTTON *towards the taxi rank.*)
  Taxi or a fly, sir?
LYTTON: Well, I don't think we ought to make too hasty a decision, do you?
  (*In the station forecourt are a couple of taxis and a row of small one-horse carriages. The* PORTER *stands, waiting for* LYTTON *to make up his mind. The various drivers are milling around.* LYTTON *scans them hastily and expertly, until his eye falls on one very handsome young man, who is standing alongside his fly.*)
  I believe I'll take that one.

3

EXT. COUNTRY TRACK. DAY
The fly bounces along a narrow country track; as it approaches, it becomes clear that LYTTON *is flirting with the* DRIVER.

EXT. ASHEHAM HOUSE. DAY
A fine, simple Georgian house, set in a hollow among fields and elms, no other houses in sight. The fly pulls up outside the house. LYTTON *pays off the* DRIVER, *tipping him, it would appear from the latter's pleased expression, rather generously.*

    The front door of the house opens and VANESSA BELL *appears in the doorway. She's thirty-six, extremely beautiful, wearing an elegantly simple long dress, which is, however, none too clean.*

    LYTTON *approaches her, drops his suitcase and kisses her.*

LYTTON: Nessa, I'm dropping.

VANESSA: The kettle's on.

    (LYTTON *walks straight past* VANESSA, *leaving her to pick up his heavy suitcase and umbrella.*)

INT. ASHEHAM HOUSE. DRAWING-ROOM. DAY
LYTTON *sweeps into the house. He drops his hat and briefcase on to the floor, and shakes hands with* CLIVE BELL.

CLIVE: Ah . . .

LYTTON: Clive.

CLIVE: I'm afraid we're fending for ourselves this weekend. The servants are off till Monday.

LYTTON: Oh, dear.

CLIVE: We've put you in the front bedroom.

VANESSA: There's a fire in the sitting-room.

LYTTON: Jolly good.

INT./EXT. SITTING-ROOM. DAY
LYTTON *heads on into the sitting-room, crossing directly to sit on a chair by the French windows;* VANESSA *follows him into the room.*

VANESSA: I'll get you a cup of tea.

LYTTON: Oh, please. Oh . . .! (*He fumbles in his breast pocket and produces a battered booklet.*) I brought you my ration cards.

VANESSA: Thanks.

    (LYTTON*'s POV: out on the lawn,* VANESSA*'s children,* JULIAN *and* QUENTIN, *are playing football with a youthful,*

4

androgynous figure, who's running with the ball in the dying light, cheeks red, blonde hair flying.)

LYTTON: Vanessa?

VANESSA: Yes.

LYTTON: Who on earth is that ravishing boy?

(VANESSA *joins him at the window, looks out at the garden, momentarily puzzled, then smiles sardonically.*)

VANESSA: I take it you're not referring to either of my sons.

LYTTON: No. (*He gets up and points.*) Him.

(*Their POV: the person he's watching kicks the ball and comes to a standstill. It's* DORA CARRINGTON*: she's twenty-two, child-like, not beautiful but striking, large, melancholy eyes, round cheeks, pale skin, shoulder-length hair cut like a Florentine pageboy and an indefinable aura of fragility.* VANESSA *smiles, opens the window and calls out.*)

VANESSA: Carrington!

(*A sharp intake of breath from* LYTTON.)

LYTTON: Good God.

VANESSA: Someone I want you to meet!

EXT. GARDEN. DAY

CARRINGTON'*s POV:* VANESSA *at the window.*

CARRINGTON: Coming! (*She runs over to let herself into the house.*)

INT. SITTING-ROOM. DAY

CARRINGTON *steps through the French windows and hesitates, momentarily intimidated by* LYTTON'*s strange appearance.*

VANESSA: This is Lytton Strachey.

(CARRINGTON *advances, her hand outstretched.*)

CARRINGTON: Hello.

(LYTTON, *still grappling with his confusion and disappointment, reluctantly accepts her hand in a limp handshake.* VANESSA *smiles, with a trace of malice and slips out of the room.*)

VANESSA: I'll fetch some tea.

LYTTON: So. You're Carrington.

CARRINGTON: Yes. (*She's watching him coolly, a shade defiantly.*)

LYTTON: Mark Gertler's friend.

CARRINGTON: Well, I know him.

LYTTON: Ah.

5

(He can't think of anything further to say. He moves over to the well-stocked bookshelves and begins intently studying their contents. She moves over to the window.

The two of them. It's a sparsely furnished room, elegantly decorated and with a number of paintings by VANESSA *and* DUNCAN GRANT. *The log fire blazes.* CARRINGTON *stares out into the garden.* LYTTON *selects a book. Silence.* CARRINGTON *gives it a moment longer and then returns to the garden.)*

INT. DRAWING-ROOM OF ASHEHAM HOUSE. NIGHT
LYTTON *is sitting in the only comfortable armchair, next to the fire, a rug spread over his knees. He is knitting a scarf.* CARRINGTON *sits in the window seat.* VANESSA *sits on a small sofa embracing her lover,* DUNCAN GRANT, *thirty, an extremely handsome and dishevelled young man. Her husband* CLIVE BELL, *thirty-four, moves around the room, puffing at a cheroot, occasionally stopping to ruffle the hair of a young blonde woman,* MARY HUTCHINSON, *twenty-six, his mistress.*

LYTTON: They'll be bringing in conscription in a matter of weeks. We shall all be dragged in front of some appalling tribunal.

MARY: You'll have to be conscientious objectors.

LYTTON: I'd rather go to prison or down the mines. It'd be warmer and I'm sure you'd meet a much nicer class of person.

BELL: Ottoline says she'll be able to help.

LYTTON: Well, there must be some compensation for having friends in high places.

*(*CARRINGTON *has been watching him. Now she speaks with scarcely disguised hostility.)*

CARRINGTON: Don't you like Ottoline?

LYTTON: I'm devoted to Ottoline. She's like the Eiffel Tower. She's very silly but she affords excellent views.

*(*CARRINGTON *looks annoyed.)*

Do you think knitting scarves for the troops would be classified as essential war work?

*(*CARRINGTON *seems about to say something, but checks herself.)*

One's so busy nowadays. I've been learning German as well. I must say, it's a most disagreeable language.

6

CARRINGTON: Then why learn it?

LYTTON: Well, my dear, I mean, suppose they win?

    (BELL *is now behind* LYTTON, *at the sideboard, where he opens a bottle of champagne.* LYTTON, *startled by the pop, lets out a high-pitched shriek.*)

Ye gods: can you imagine what the war must be like?

    (CARRINGTON'*s cheeks are red with indignation.*)

EXT. SUSSEX DOWNS. DAY

Clear, windy day. CLIVE BELL *and* MARY HUTCHINSON *pass, arm-in-arm. Then, a few yards behind,* DUNCAN GRANT *and* VANESSA. *Finally, some yards behind them, somewhat stiffly bringing up the rear,* LYTTON *and* CARRINGTON. LYTTON *gestures towards the two couples ahead.*

LYTTON: I must say, as Nessa and Clive are both having affairs with cousins of mine, I can't help thinking theirs is a peculiarly civilized marriage.

    (CARRINGTON *glances at him, somewhat disapprovingly and doesn't answer. He decides to try a different tack.*)

Do you really like to be called Carrington?

CARRINGTON: Yes.

LYTTON: Why?

CARRINGTON: My first name is Dora.

LYTTON: Ah, I see.

    (*They stop for a moment to contemplate the view. Below them, deserted fields roll away to the coast. In the distance, the dull gleam of the Channel, iron-grey and flat. There's a strange sound in the air, a barely audible rumble, as of some remote thunderstorm.*)

CARRINGTON: Can you hear them?

LYTTON: What?

CARRINGTON: The guns.

LYTTON: Oh, yes.

    (*They stand a moment, listening.*)

CARRINGTON: I have three brothers over there.

LYTTON: I can't tell you how angry it makes me feel.

CARRINGTON: I'd have joined up, if I'd been a man.

LYTTON: But surely you don't believe . . .

CARRINGTON: Of course not, of course I don't believe in it. But

I'd still have joined up.
(*The others have disappeared on ahead. Silence, except for the guns.*)
I wish I'd been born a boy.
(LYTTON *is momentarily disconcerted by her intensity. Then, he smiles.*)
LYTTON: You have such lovely ears.
(*Suddenly,* LYTTON *puts his gloved hands round the back of* CARRINGTON'*s head, stoops and kisses her on the lips. She resists, violently struggling.*)
CARRINGTON: Don't. Stop it!
(LYTTON *releases her.*)
Would you mind not!
LYTTON: Sorry.
(*They stand a moment longer,* LYTTON *sheepish,* CARRINGTON *furious. Then they turn more or less simultaneously and set off up the hill without a word.*)

INT. LANDING IN ASHEHAM HOUSE. DAWN
CARRINGTON *tiptoes along the landing. She carries a large pair of kitchen scissors.*
   She stops outside a door, hesitates, then opens the door with extreme care and lets herself into LYTTON'*s bedroom.*

INT. BEDROOM IN ASHEHAM HOUSE. DAWN
LYTTON *is in bed, asleep. He's lying on his back, his beard outside the covers.*
   CARRINGTON *tiptoes over to him. She leans over him, gently lifts his beard and tucks it in between the blades of the scissors; then, suddenly struck by something about him, she freezes in the very act of operating the scissors.*
   LYTTON *opens his eyes and smiles at her.*
LYTTON: Have you brought my breakfast?
CARRINGTON: No, I haven't.
(LYTTON *suddenly becomes aware of the scissors, exhibits a trace of alarm.*)
I was going to cut your beard off.
(LYTTON *stares at her, perplexed, as she carefully withdraws the scissors.*)

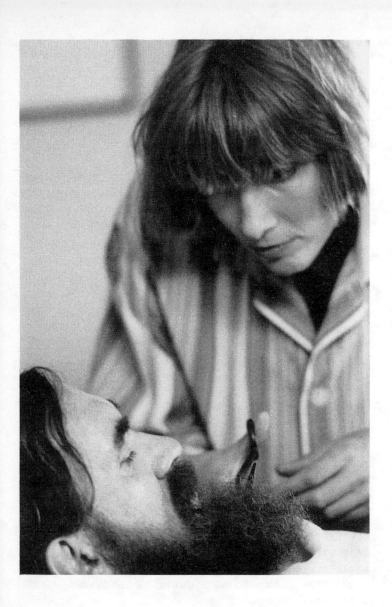

LYTTON: Why?

CARRINGTON: To punish you.

LYTTON: Oh, I see.

CARRINGTON: Yes.

    (LYTTON *smiles. He seems to find the whole situation exhilarating. He plucks briefly at his beard.* CARRINGTON *is still staring at him like a frightened rabbit.*)

LYTTON: And do you still want to punish me?

CARRINGTON: No. No, I don't.

    FADE

CAPTION ON BLACK SCREEN

TWO

GERTLER 1916–1918

EXT./INT. GERTLER'S STUDIO. NIGHT

Sounds of struggle. The studio consists of a strange passage-like glass structure erected against a wall and leading into a kind of garden shed which serves as Gertler's bedroom. CARRINGTON *and* GERTLER, *apparently engaged in a kind of amorous dance, grapple the length of the studio.*

INT. GERTLER'S BEDROOM. NIGHT

GERTLER *manhandles the struggling* CARRINGTON *through the door and over to the bed, on to which they collapse and flounder around for a time.* GERTLER *is an intense, slight, dark man of twenty-four, whose excessive energy gives off a strong whiff of banked-down violence.*

CARRINGTON: Enough. That's enough!

    (*She smacks at his hand and sits up, straightening her dress.* GERTLER *sighs impatiently.*)

GERTLER: Why?

CARRINGTON: I'll have to go soon, anyway.

GERTLER: Why don't you stay the night?

CARRINGTON: Look, let's not go through all this again.

GERTLER: I'm only asking.

CARRINGTON: It makes me think you're only interested in me sexually.

    (GERTLER *springs to his feet, enraged.*)

GERTLER: You make me so angry. Of course I'm interested in you sexually. But I'm not *only* interested in you sexually. I can get that anywhere. I'm interested in you, your opinions, your work, what you think of me, so naturally I'm interested in you sexually as well. What do you expect? I did ask you to marry me, for God's sake.

CARRINGTON: I know, Mark, but . . .

GERTLER: I'd understand if you thought I was ugly. If you thought I was ugly, you wouldn't like me at all and you say you do.

CARRINGTON: Of course I do.

GERTLER: Well, then . . .

CARRINGTON: It's you I like, not your body.

GERTLER: I am my body.

CARRINGTON: Goodnight.

(CARRINGTON *picks up her coat, turns and opens the studio door, and hurries out into the night.* GERTLER *calls after her.*)

GERTLER: You can't expect to stay a virgin all your life.

INT. GERTLER'S STUDIO. DAY

CARRINGTON *sits, modelling for* GERTLER *in a plain blue dress.*
GERTLER *applies the paint to his canvas with a delicate brush and a series of precise, almost finicky strokes. He looks up and frowns.*

GERTLER: What's the matter?

CARRINGTON: I was just thinking about that disgusting old man with a beard.

GERTLER: I really shouldn't brood about it if I were you. After all, he's a bugger.

CARRINGTON: What?

GERTLER: Lytton. He's a bugger.

CARRINGTON: I never know what that means.

(GERTLER *sighs, exasperated.*)

GERTLER: He's a homosexual.

(CARRINGTON *nods sagely; but she's evidently none the wiser.*)

INT. ANTE-ROOM IN HAMPSTEAD TOWN HALL

LYTTON *sits on a bench, isolated, his rug around his knees, waiting, lit from above through a municipal stained-glass window, reading a stout volume.*

INT. COURTROOM IN HAMPSTEAD TOWN HALL. DAY

CARRINGTON *slips unobtrusively into the chamber in which the Hampstead Conscription Tribunal is in session. She sits on her own at the back of the gloomy room unnoticed by* GERTLER *who sits at the front with* CLIVE *and* VANESSA BELL, DUNCAN GRANT *and* MARY HUTCHINSON, *whose comparative youth and unconventional appearance seem at odds with the general atmosphere. The tribunal itself, its eight* MEMBERS *seated behind a long table, includes the* MAYOR *(in full regalia) and the uniformed* MILITARY REPRESENTATIVE. *In the main body of the room, a few elderly members of the general public. The* USHER *is crossing to open the doors to the courtroom.*

MAYOR: (*Voiceover*) Call Mr Strachey!

USHER: Giles Lytton Strachey!

> (*It is not* LYTTON, *however, who enters, but a dignified and impressive figure, formally dressed, carrying an uninflated light brown air cushion. This is* PHILIP MORRELL, *forty-six.*
> The MAYOR *looks up at* MORRELL, *shadow of a frown.*)

MAYOR: Mr Strachey?

MORRELL: No. Philip Morrell.

> (*Impressive pause.*)

> M.P. for Burnley.

> (*He carefully sets down the air cushion on the empty chair in the centre of the room.*)

MAYOR: Erm . . .

MORRELL: I believe Mr Strachey is marshalling his documents.

> (*At this moment* LYTTON *blunders into the room, wearing his overcoat and carrying a tartan rug, a Homburg, an ancient briefcase, a volume of Gibbon and an umbrella. He walks through the court towards the empty chair. He hooks his umbrella on the back of the chair, drops his briefcase on the floor and folds the rug over the arm of the chair. He then takes off his hat, scarf and coat and lets them fall either side of the chair.*
> CARRINGTON *is watching intently from the back of the room.*)

MAYOR: Mr Strachey.

> (LYTTON *raises an enormously long finger.*)

LYTTON: One moment. (*He takes the air cushion from the chair, unscrews its stopper and proceeds, with some effort and far from silently, to inflate it.*)

12

(*The* MAYOR *and* MEMBERS *of the Tribunal watch him, transfixed.* LYTTON *finishes inflating the cushion, puts it down on the chair and lowers himself cautiously on to it. Then he looks up.*)
I'm a martyr to the piles.
(*The* MAYOR*'s face is swept by contradictory emotions. He swallows, clears his throat, consults his papers.*)
MAYOR: You are a . . . writer by profession, is that correct?
LYTTON: It is. I am.
MAYOR: Now, according to this report from the Advisory Committee, you've made a statement to the effect that you have a conscientious objection to taking part in the war.
(*He pauses.* LYTTON, *however, doesn't answer.*)
Did you make such a statement?
LYTTON: Yes.
(*The* MILITARY REPRESENTATIVE, *who has had difficulty in controlling his impatience, now intervenes.*)
MILITARY REPRESENTATIVE: Mr Strachey.
LYTTON: Yes.
MILITARY REPRESENTATIVE: Are we to understand that you have a conscientious objection to all wars?
LYTTON: Oh, no. Not at all. Only this one.
(*Silence. Then the* MILITARY REPRESENTATIVE *unleashes his prize question.*)
MILITARY REPRESENTATIVE: Then, would you care to tell us what you would do if you saw a German soldier raping your sister?
(LYTTON *considers a moment, then speaks with the utmost deadpan seriousness.*)
LYTTON: I believe I should attempt to come between them.
(*Laughter in the court. The* MAYOR *passes a hand in front of his eyes. He's caught by surprise as* LYTTON *leans forward and speaks with a quiet intensity.*)
I will not assist, by any deliberate action of mine, in carrying on this war. My objection is based not upon religious belief, but upon moral considerations; and I will not act against these convictions, whatever the consequences may be.
(*There's a round of applause from his friends; and* CARRINGTON, *somewhat to her own surprise, finds herself joining in.*)

EXT. HAMPSTEAD HEATH. DAY

Spring day. GERTLER *crosses the Heath with* LYTTON, *swathed in coat, scarf, Homburg, gloves and galoshes, drained by the proceedings of the Tribunal.*

LYTTON: Well, after all that, the prospect of jail seems positively soothing.

GERTLER: They'll never send you to jail. Too many of them went to school with you.

LYTTON: I only hope you're right. (*He darts a shrewd glance at* GERTLER.) Any luck with the famous Carrington conundrum?

GERTLER: It's only ignorance. Fear and ignorance. But it's been going on for four years. I'm at my wits' end.

LYTTON: Well, it's no good asking my opinion. I'm afraid when it comes to a creature with a cunt I'm always infinitely *désorienté.*

GERTLER: All the same, I've decided, if anyone can help me, you can.

INT. GERTLER'S STUDIO. DAY

LYTTON *perches uncomfortably on a wooden chair, sipping a mug of tea, huddled up against a paraffin stove, having retained every item of clothing except his hat.* GERTLER *is on his feet. On an easel, as yet unfinished, is* GERTLER's *painting, 'The Merry-Go-Round', subsequently to become his most famous canvas, a harsh, stylized study of men, mostly uniformed, and women, astride wooden horses, frozen in sinister and joyless pleasure.*

LYTTON: I? How?

GERTLER: Well, I don't know exactly. I mean if you just *be* with her a little. A man like you, she has no older friends, you see, she's bound to learn.

LYTTON: Keats' letters, of course, are very poignant on the subject of virginity.

GERTLER: And my work.

LYTTON: What?

(GERTLER *waves an arm at 'The Merry-Go-Round'.*)

GERTLER: Take this, for example. This is a radical painting. This is my statement about the soulless mechanisms of war. She won't understand that. The harmonies, for example, they're like Bach, don't you agree?

(LYTTON *contemplates the painting, alarmed, searching for an appropriate response.*)

LYTTON: But, the critics . . . I mean, surely nowadays the papers are full of nothing but Gertler.

GERTLER: That's no good to her. Someone must explain to her, someone she respects, that I'm an important artist.

LYTTON: And you think if she realizes that, she'll . . .

GERTLER: I'm sure of it.

INT. CARRINGTON'S STUDIO AT 2 GOWER STREET. EVENING
Close on LYTTON.

LYTTON: To begin with, I'm still compelled, at my advanced age, to live in my mother's house, simply because I'm more or less *sans le sou*. You probably think of me as a man of letters, but all I've ever managed to publish is a few reviews and a slim volume of criticism. I can't write half the things I want to write; and if I did, I wouldn't dare publish them, for fear of killing my mother.

(*During this, the camera has tracked slowly back to reveal that* LYTTON *is lying on a chaise-longue, holding a large book. A tartan rug covers him.* CARRINGTON *is eventually revealed at her easel; she's working on a portrait in oils, concentrating fiercely.*)

Furthermore, I now find myself, despite my great age and notorious health, being harassed by the government to go off and take part in some entirely ridiculous war they seem quite unable to grasp is resulting in large numbers of people dying. So I'm now reduced to the degrading task of writing pamphlets for the No-Conscription Fellowship which may very possibly land me in prison. In other words, I'm obscure, decrepit, terrified, ill-favoured, penniless and fond of adjectives.

(CARRINGTON *looks up, smiling.*)

CARRINGTON: Surely it's not that bad.

LYTTON: No, no. You're quite right, looked at another way, I'm a perfectly respectable elderly bugger of modest means.

(CARRINGTON *laughs, pausing in her work. She glances out of the window.*)

CARRINGTON: I suppose you ought to be going soon, before it gets dark.

LYTTON: Oh, no, no, no, I adore the blackout, the most thrilling encounters . . . you mustn't deny us our few simple pleasures, dear, after all, we've not much else to look forward to, except old age.

(CARRINGTON *resumes painting. Silence.*)

LYTTON: Dear God, can you imagine it? The rain, the loneliness, the regret.

CARRINGTON: No, I can't imagine it.

LYTTON: Well, you just wait till it's staring you in the face.

CARRINGTON: How old are you, anyway?

LYTTON: I'm thirty-six next birthday.

(CARRINGTON *smiles, carries on painting.*)

Ottoline's invited me up to Garsington next weekend.

EXT. GARSINGTON MANOR. DAY

Beautiful spring day. The back of Garsington Manor house, a two-storeyed Jacobean mansion built of Cotswold stone, leading into 200 acres of the Berkshire downs. The gardens, at present empty, except for two or three elderly GARDENERS *and a sprinkling of* GUESTS *on the croquet lawn, are spectacularly designed and maintained.*

CARRINGTON: (*Voiceover*) Me too.

LYTTON: (*Voiceover*) Oh. I'll go if you go. Last time I was there, everyone was either deaf or French.

INT. LYTTON'S BEDROOM AT GARSINGTON. DAY

LYTTON *is dressing. He's almost finished putting on his trousers, when an extraordinary figure sweeps into the room without knocking.*

  It is LADY OTTOLINE MORRELL, *a woman of strikingly eccentric appearance, swathed in an astonishing, trailing peach silk dress and wearing a preposterous matching hat. She's forty-two and her beaky nose and prognathous jaw give her face an alternately regal and ridiculous expression which is heightened by bizarrely and lavishly applied make-up.* LYTTON *struggles with his fly buttons, exhibiting a faint trace of annoyance.*

OTTOLINE: Well? How is the campaign proceeding?

(LYTTON *frowns, bemused.* OTTOLINE *has produced a humbug from somewhere, which she pops into her mouth and sucks noisily.*)

LYTTON: Campaign?

OTTOLINE: The Carrington matter. I take it you're still working on her.

LYTTON: Really Ottoline, must you put things quite so baldly. I prefer to think of myself as an educator rather than a . . .

OTTOLINE: A what?

LYTTON: A pimp.

OTTOLINE: Now, don't be silly, you know as well as I do, it's a sickness with Carrington. A girl of that age, still a virgin, it's absurd.

LYTTON: I was still a virgin at that age.

OTTOLINE: But that's my whole point, don't you see, so was I. Is there to be no progress?

(*And with this, she sweeps out of the room.*)

EXT. FORMAL GARDENS AT GARSINGTON MANOR. DAY

CARRINGTON *moves disconsolately through the gardens in* OTTOLINE*'s wake.*

OTTOLINE: Now I must have a serious talk to you before Mark arrives.

(*Despite the heat,* OTTOLINE *is entirely wrapped in a heavy black cloak and wears a three-cornered hat, so that she looks like some demented highwayman. She is attended by several snuffling pugs.*)

I know how difficult it is, my dear, to reconcile puritanism with a love of beauty. It's a consideration that's never far from my thoughts when I'm in Burnley.

(CARRINGTON *opens her mouth to protest, but* OTTOLINE *surges on.*)

I mean, take this garden, for example. Surely it wouldn't be right to plant nothing but cabbages and cauliflowers? Or do you think it's wanton or wicked of us to love the bastard tulip or the Turk's Head lily?

CARRINGTON: Of course not, no.

(OTTOLINE *interrupts her with a wagging finger.*)

OTTOLINE: One can't have it all ways. Remember that! And I firmly believe it's high time you took the bull by the horns.

(CARRINGTON *turns away and hurries along the grass path.* OTTOLINE *is unaware that* CARRINGTON *is no longer following her.*)

18

We can't always live under glass like a cucumber. We have to engage with life!

EXT. GARSINGTON MANOR TERRACE. DAY

CARRINGTON *runs up the steps towards the terrace where she is unable to avoid being intercepted by* PHILIP MORRELL.

MORRELL: Ah, there you are, Carrington. I was hoping to find an opportunity to talk to you in private before Mark's arrival.
(MORRELL *takes her by the arm and leads her into the house.*)

CARRINGTON: (*Voiceover*) And then, would you believe it, Pipsey harangued me for half-an-hour on the perils of virginity.

EXT. ROOF OF GARSINGTON MANOR. DAY

LYTTON *listens to* CARRINGTON, *amused, propped against a gable. Below, oblivious, visitors move through the formal gardens.*

CARRINGTON: He got more and more breathy and the hairs in his nostrils became horribly agitated. Finally, he told me it was someone like me had driven his brother Hugh to suicide.

LYTTON: Ah, semen. What is it about that ridiculous white secretion that pulls down the corners of an Englishman's mouth?
(*Silence.* CARRINGTON *broods for a moment.*)

CARRINGTON: You see, I'm not against it in theory. It's just the thought of Mark somehow.

LYTTON: Well, I can't, of course, agree with you, but there we are.

EXT. WITTENHAM CLUMPS. DAY

A clump of old elms, surmounting a hill. LYTTON *sits up, leaning against one of the trees, his panama hat very straight on his head. Beside him,* CARRINGTON *is stretched out, lying on her stomach, chin in her hands, her long, cheap dress pulled up slightly to show her short white socks and child's shoes. The countryside is spread out below them. Silence.*

CARRINGTON: Lytton.
(LYTTON *doesn't answer, turns his head to her. She reaches up and takes his hand.*)
I love being with you.

(*Again,* LYTTON *doesn't answer, except for a vague smile.*)
You're so cold and wise.
(LYTTON *frowns, slightly perplexed.*)
These last few months, whenever I know I'm going to see you, I get so excited inside.
(LYTTON *watches her.*)
If you were to kiss me again, I don't think I'd mind at all.
(*Silence.*)

LYTTON: You know, it's a strange thing, but I'd rather like to.
(*He leans down to her and kisses her briefly on the lips. His hat falls off. She smiles up at him and he stretches himself out and kisses her again.*)

CARRINGTON: Your skin is like ivory. (*She kisses him again, quickly, and then snuggles into the crook of his arm.*)
That day I came in, you remember, to cut your beard off. I knew then.
(LYTTON *disengages his arm, sits up, puts his hat on, wraps his arms around his knees.*)

LYTTON: I don't think this is what Mark had in mind at all.

CARRINGTON: He's not to know.

LYTTON: All the same, I can't help feeling rather shifty.
(*Longish silence.* CARRINGTON *sits up on one elbow.*)

21

CARRINGTON: What I knew was, was that I was in love with you.
(LYTTON *looks down at her, surprised. Then he smiles at her, touched, and reaches across to stroke her cheek.*)

EXT. GARDENS AT GARSINGTON. EVENING
Towards sunset. LYTTON *and* CARRINGTON *move hand in hand across the lawns. In the distance, the sound of a harmonium playing 'When This Lousy War Is Over'.*
LYTTON: I heard from the Military Doctors' Board this morning. They've rejected me. Medically unfit for any kind of service.
CARRINGTON: But, Lytton, that's wonderful.
LYTTON: Wonderful for me.
(*They pass through an archway in a hedge and stop.* LYTTON *lets go of* CARRINGTON*'s hand. The harmonium modulates to a jaunty variation of the same tune.*

Below them, on a sunken lawn not far from the house, OTTOLINE*'s party is in full swing.* MORRELL *is pumping away at the treadle of the harmonium, sweating profusely in his high, stiff collar. All the other* GUESTS *are dancing. Several of them have been kitted out with Oriental costumes from* OTTOLINE*'s wardrobe.* OTTOLINE *herself is wearing an outrageous Bakstian costume with a turban to match. The dancing is strangely modern, the dancers in couples but moving independently to the music as the fancy takes them.*

LYTTON *and* CARRINGTON *stand, looking down at the tableau.*)
LYTTON: Thousands of boys are dying every day to preserve this, did you know?
CARRINGTON: Yes.
(LYTTON *watches. A spasm of something very like passion contorts his face for a moment.*)
LYTTON: Goddamn, blast, confound and fuck the upper classes.
(*The dancers leap and jig, lurid in the reddening light.* LYTTON *shakes his head.*)
Let's see if we can't avoid all this, shall we, and go and read some Rimbaud.
(*They disappear back through the arch as the dancers pound on, oblivious.*)

22

EXT. LAKE AT GARSINGTON. DAY

GERTLER, *faintly ludicrous in a striped bathing costume, hauls himself out of the lake, his expression fierce and embittered and flops down next to* CARRINGTON, *going straight on to the attack as if pursuing some argument.*

GERTLER: You're the lady, I'm the Jew-boy from the East End, that's it, isn't it?

CARRINGTON: Of course not.

GERTLER: I don't know why you don't admit it!

CARRINGTON: Because it's not true.

    (GERTLER *stares at her, unbelieving.*)

    You don't understand. I need my freedom.

GERTLER: Freedom? How can you have any freedom when you're frightened to use your body?

CARRINGTON: You must have patience.

GERTLER: What do you mean, patience? It is killing me all this, it is killing me.

CARRINGTON: I'm sorry.

GERTLER: Think how much your body has deteriorated in the past four years, all that time wasted.

CARRINGTON: Keats' letters . . .

    (GERTLER *interrupts her, shouting.*)

GERTLER: Don't talk to me about Keats, what the hell use is Keats to me?

    (CARRINGTON *maintains a stubborn silence as* GERTLER *flounces away, throwing down his towel.*)

EXT. GARSINGTON MANOR TERRACE. DAY

GERTLER *sits on a low wall, sketching* LYTTON, *who's taking his ease in a wicker armchair, nursing a glass of wine.*

LYTTON: I have a suggestion.

GERTLER: What?

LYTTON: I'm planning a couple of weeks' holiday in Wales. Why don't I take her with me?

    (GERTLER *looks up, surprised, a touch suspicious.*)

    You see, I've been teaching her French. We're about to get on to the French poets, I've a feeling they may prove decisive.

    (GERTLER *frowns, still dubious.*)

CARRINGTON *stands on a hillock, facing out to sea, painting. She's wearing corduroy trousers and a green shirt. Presently* LYTTON *appears round the hill: he looks dashingly eccentric and moves with an unwonted spring in his step. He comes up to* CARRINGTON *and looks at her landscape for a moment.*

LYTTON: I've come to the sad conclusion there's no such thing as a beautiful Welsh boy. At any rate, I've seen nothing but the most unparalleled frumps.

CARRINGTON: But wouldn't it be lovely to live in the country? I'm sick of towns.

LYTTON: Yes. (*He reflects for a moment.*) Perhaps we should set up house together.

(CARRINGTON *stops painting and looks up at him, surprised and delighted.* LYTTON *is already regretting his impulsiveness.*)

CARRINGTON: Do you really mean that?

LYTTON: Well yes . . . I did . . . yes.

(CARRINGTON *considers.* LYTTON *watches her, in suspense.*)

CARRINGTON: No, I don't think so.

(LYTTON *looks unmistakably relieved.*)

LYTTON: Probably just as well. Anyway, I couldn't afford it.

CARRINGTON: I see.

LYTTON: I'm sorry. I tend to be rather impulsive in these matters. Like the time I asked Virginia Woolf to marry me.

CARRINGTON: She turned you down?

LYTTON: No, no, she accepted. It was ghastly.

(*Silence.* CARRINGTON *is hurt.*)

CARRINGTON: And if I'd accepted, I suppose that would have been ghastly?

LYTTON: No, I don't think it would.

INT. BOARDING-HOUSE BEDROOM. NIGHT

A plain country bedroom with twin beds. LYTTON *sits up in his bed, taking pills and washing them down with a glass of water.* CARRINGTON *is pulling on her pyjama bottoms, somewhat inadequately concealed by an open wardrobe door.* LYTTON *pretends not to watch.*

CARRINGTON: What's that you're taking?

LYTTON: Dr Gregory's Rhubarb Pills. I find them sovereign.

(CARRINGTON *ties her pyjamas, starts off towards her bed,*
hesitates fractionally. LYTTON *smiles at her.*)
One bed is warmer than two.
(CARRINGTON *crosses quickly to* LYTTON's *bed and climbs in.*
He kisses her. Then he draws his head back and they look at
each other. CARRINGTON *speaks very quietly.*)
CARRINGTON: Anything you like, Lytton. Anything.
(*Silence. Then* LYTTON *smiles apologetically.*)
LYTTON: It's all very well . . . (*He breaks off, strokes her cheek.*)
CARRINGTON: It doesn't matter. (*She turns her head away from*
him so he can't see her face.) Really it doesn't.
(LYTTON *smiles again, wistfully, strokes her hair, leans over and*
tenderly kisses her ear. She thinks for a moment and puts her
arm down under the covers. LYTTON *raises his eyebrows.*
CARRINGTON's *arm starts to move.* LYTTON *closes his eyes.*)

INT. LYTTON'S STUDY AT 6, BELSIZE PARK GARDENS. EVENING
A rather formal, gloomy room. LYTTON *sits in his armchair by the*
fire, a rug over his knees and a glass of Sanatogen at his elbow.
CARRINGTON *is moving around the room, worried and thoughtful.*
CARRINGTON: Mark's borrowed Gilbert Cannan's house at
    Cholesbury. He wants me to spend a few days with him.
LYTTON: Then you must go.
CARRINGTON: I'm not sure I want to.
LYTTON: Then you mustn't go.
CARRINGTON: Can't you see, Lytton, I'm asking you to help me.
LYTTON: My dear, as we both know, I'm supposed to be
    bringing you together . . .

INT. DRAWING-ROOM IN THE WINDMILL AT CHOLESBURY. NIGHT
GERTLER *sits alone, in front of a dying fire, waiting. He gulps down*
a glass of wine. Finally, he gets up and leaves the room, taking the
oil lamp with him.
LYTTON: (*Voiceover*) . . . but in these matters, in these matters
    above all, you really have to make your own decisions.

INT. STAIRCASE AND LANDING IN THE WINDMILL. NIGHT
GERTLER *climbs the stairs slowly, lighting his way with the lamp. He*
moves down the landing, comes to a halt outside a door which is

slightly ajar. He waits a second before speaking.
GERTLER: Ready?
> (CARRINGTON *answers, panic in her voice, from inside the room.*)

CARRINGTON: (*Off-screen*) It's too big, Mark, I can't get it in, I've
tried and tried, but I can't.
> (GERTLER *starts to push the door open.*)

(*Off-screen*) Don't come in!
> (GERTLER *goes in, closing the door behind him.*)

EXT. THE WINDMILL. NIGHT
The house, lit by moonlight. Deep silence. Then, inside the house,
CARRINGTON *cries out.*

INT. BEDROOM IN THE WINDMILL. NIGHT
The room is strangely lit by the oil lamp, which GERTLER *has left on
the floor. He is making love to* CARRINGTON, *violently.*
   CARRINGTON's *face is contorted with fear and disgust. Her eyes are
tightly shut. Tears squeeze out of the corners of her eyes.*

INT. QUEEN'S HALL. EVENING
Schubert's Quintet in C.
   CARRINGTON *is in the audience, sitting next to* LYTTON. *Tears run
down her cheeks. She turns and whispers to* LYTTON.
CARRINGTON: Lytton.
LYTTON: Yes.
CARRINGTON: What you said about us living together in the
country.
LYTTON: Yes.
CARRINGTON: Did you really mean it?
> (LYTTON *is pensive a moment. Then he turns to her.*)

LYTTON: Yes.

EXT. COUNTRY ROAD IN OXFORDSHIRE. DAY
CARRINGTON *cycles down a deserted country lane.*

EXT. RECTORY IN BERKSHIRE. DAY
CARRINGTON *cycles up the front drive of a red-brick rectory.*

EXT. SMALL MANOR HOUSE IN OXFORDSHIRE. DAY
CARRINGTON *scrambles up a bank to look over the gate at the Georgian house.*

EXT. THE MILL HOUSE AT TIDMARSH. DAY
The back garden of the Mill House, a pleasant six-bedroom house, with the mill stream running under it. The garden is secluded and consists of a large lawn, an orchard, several yew trees, a greenhouse, a vegetable garden and an old shed. LYTTON *stands, looking up at the house, hands in pockets.* CARRINGTON *is standing beside a small sunken bath, full of old leaves and debris at the moment, but kept fairly clear by the mill stream which flows through it.*
LYTTON: Yes, but a pound a week. I don't see how I can manage it.
CARRINGTON: Our own Roman bath, look.
LYTTON: Most hygienic.

INT. LARGE BEDROOM IN THE MILL HOUSE. DAY
LYTTON *stands in the middle of the room, which is entirely bare, looking suspiciously at the peeling walls There's dust everywhere.*
CARRINGTON: And this will be your room.
(LYTTON's *expression is profoundly dubious.*)
And electric light in every room, look.
LYTTON: Yes, that is a blessing.
CARRINGTON: Now, don't worry, by the time I've finished with it, you won't recognize it.
(LYTTON's *on his way to the door, covering his mouth with his handkerchief.*)
LYTTON: Hm.

INT. TOUR EIFFEL RESTAURANT IN CHARLOTTE STREET. EVENING
CARRINGTON *and* GERTLER *face each other across a half-eaten meal.*
GERTLER: Are you going to live with him?
CARRINGTON: No. I just felt I had to tell him I was in love with him.
GERTLER: What did he say?
CARRINGTON: He said he was sorry.
(GERTLER *laughs incredulously.*)
GERTLER: Is that all?

27

CARRINGTON: Well, it's not his fault. What else could he say?
  (*Silence.* GERTLER *stares at her for a moment, speaks quietly.*)
GERTLER: I never want to see you again. So would you mind if I left you directly after dinner?
CARRINGTON: No.
  (*Another pause. Then, suddenly,* GERTLER *crashes his knife and fork down on the plate and shouts at her.*)
GERTLER: I've always said life was a crooked business! To think after all these years . . . to fall in love with a man like Strachey . . . twice your age . . . (*He breaks off, jumps to his feet and stumbles out of the restaurant.*)
CARRINGTON: (*Voiceover*) I thought I'd better tell Mark, as it was so difficult going on.
LYTTON: (*Voiceover*) Tell him what?

INT. CARRINGTON'S STUDIO IN GOWER STREET. NIGHT
LYTTON *sits in the armchair in front of the fire.* CARRINGTON *paces up and down.*
CARRINGTON: That it couldn't go on. So I told him. I told him I was in love with you.
  (*Silence.* LYTTON *looks at her, dismayed.*)
LYTTON: Aren't you being rather romantic? Are you certain?
  (CARRINGTON *smiles.*)
CARRINGTON: There's nothing romantic about it.
LYTTON: What did Mark say?
CARRINGTON: He was terribly upset.
LYTTON: It's all too incongruous. I'm so old and diseased, I wish I was more . . . able.
CARRINGTON: It doesn't matter.
  (CARRINGTON *kneels in front of* LYTTON. *Silence.* LYTTON *is still perplexed.*)
LYTTON: What do you think we ought to do about the physical?
CARRINGTON: I don't mind about that.
LYTTON: Ah. But you should.
  (*Silence.*)
CARRINGTON: All this is quite deliberate, you know.
  (*Silence.*)
LYTTON: I wish I was rich, then I could keep you as my mistress.
  (CARRINGTON *looks up at him, angrily.*)

28

CARRINGTON: What difference would that make?
> (*Silence. Then,* LYTTON *gets down on his knees and takes her hands. She looks up at him a moment, then releases her hands, gets up on her knees, takes hold of his beard and kisses him passionately. They kneel there, swaying a moment, then break apart.*)
Will you stay?
LYTTON: Well . . . I . . .
CARRINGTON: Won't you spoil me? Just this once, tonight?

EXT. LONDON STREETS. NIGHT
LYTTON *strides through the darkness of the blackout, head bowed.*

INT. CARRINGTON'S STUDIO. NIGHT
The half-finished portrait of LYTTON, *only just visible in the darkness: the sound of* CARRINGTON *weeping. She's sitting alone on the* chaise longue.

EXT. THE MILL HOUSE. DAY
CARRINGTON *is up a ladder, painting the window frames.*

INT. LYTTON'S BEDROOM IN THE MILL HOUSE. DAY
CARRINGTON *is decorating Lytton's bedroom.*

EXT. FRONT OF THE MILL HOUSE. DAY
There's a green pantechnicon pulled up outside the house and CARRINGTON *is supervising a number of* WORKMEN, *who carry furniture in through the front door.*

EXT. MILL HOUSE. DAY
CARRINGTON *runs to greet* LYTTON, *who's just paying off a taxi, which pulls away, revealing two large suitcases and a cardboard box containing about twenty light bulbs. Having pecked* CARRINGTON *on the cheek,* LYTTON, *after the briefest hesitation, picks up his box of bulbs and sets off down the slope, leaving* CARRINGTON *to struggle after him with both cases. He shows her the box of bulbs.*
LYTTON: I come bearing gifts.
CARRINGTON: Oh! Globes.
LYTTON: Looted from Mother's.

CARRINGTON: What a hero. If I were bigger, I'd carry you across the threshold.

(LYTTON *smiles, but he's clearly very apprehensive. He steps gingerly into the house.*)

INT. HALLWAY IN THE MILL HOUSE. DAY
Chaos. Dust sheets, paint pots, bookcases, a ladder. And so on.
LYTTON *advances down the hallway with some difficulty.*
LYTTON: Well done!

(*He reaches for the handle of a closed door.* CARRINGTON, *who's started off up the stairs, drops the suitcases in alarm.*)
CARRINGTON: Don't go in there!

(LYTTON *frowns briefly at her, then opens the door.*)

INT. DOWNSTAIRS ROOM IN THE MILL HOUSE. DAY
LYTTON'*s POV: an indescribable mess. Apart from anything else, the room is two inches deep in water.*

INT. HALLWAY AND STAIRCASE. DAY
LYTTON *turns to look at* CARRINGTON, *appalled.*
CARRINGTON: The pipes seized up. Then they burst.
LYTTON: Good God!

CARRINGTON: Come upstairs.
> (LYTTON, *his expression profoundly gloomy, plods across the hall and starts off up the stairs after* CARRINGTON, *bumping his head on a low beam.*)

INT. LYTTON'S BEDROOM IN THE MILL HOUSE. DAY
CARRINGTON *has painted Lytton's room with a representation of the Garden of Eden. The huge figure of Adam faces, further down the wall, the only slightly less huge figure of Eve. There's a fire burning in the grate and the bedcovers have been turned back to accommodate three hot-water bottles.* CARRINGTON *nervously shepherds* LYTTON *into the room. He stands in the doorway, looking around the room in amazement.* CARRINGTON *waits, his suitcases in her hands, on tenterhooks.*
LYTTON: It's remarkable!
> (CARRINGTON, *immensely relieved, finally puts down the suitcases.*)

INT. DINING-ROOM OF THE HUTCHINSONS' HOUSE IN
HAMMERSMITH. NIGHT
The room is crowded with GUESTS, *eating a buffet supper. In a corner of the room,* LYTTON *has managed to secure a chair and sits, eating. Around him, squeezed into uncomfortable positions by the crowd, are* CLIVE BELL *and* MARY HUTCHINSON. CARRINGTON *squats at his feet, eating.*
LYTTON: Yes, it seems that *Eminent Victorians* is about to burst upon an astonished world.
MARY: That's marvellous, Lytton.
BELL: And not before time.
LYTTON: Chatto and Windus claim to find it enchanting. It's not absolutely the adjective I had in mind, but I . . .
> (*He breaks off as a plate crashes to the ground.* GERTLER *has appeared in the doorway, pale and haggard, and has barged into one of the* GUESTS. *He,* LYTTON *and* CARRINGTON *are immediately aware of each other.*
> *Ignoring the protests of the man he has bumped into,* GERTLER *pushes over to the corner and, without a word, seizes* CARRINGTON'*s wrist, drags her up, upsetting her plate and pulls her over to the door.*)

31

INT. HALL AND STAIRCASE IN THE HUTCHINSONS' HOUSE. NIGHT
CARRINGTON *struggles to free her wrist, but* GERTLER, *his face grim
and set, drags her across the hall and up the stairs.* GUESTS *stop in
their tracks and stare, open-mouthed. At the top of the stairs*
GERTLER *stands for a moment staring at* CARRINGTON, *panting
slightly. His movements are unsteady.*
   CARRINGTON *watches him, tense but apparently calm.*
GERTLER: You're living with him!
CARRINGTON: Yes.
   (GERTLER *explodes, shouting at her.*)
GERTLER: How could you lie to me like that? Did you think I
   wouldn't find out?
CARRINGTON: I didn't want to hurt you.
   (GERTLER *gives a snort of bitter laughter.*)
GERTLER: Do you know, when I found out, just thinking about
   you and that half-dead eunuch, I vomited all night. You've
   poisoned my life. Haven't you any self-respect?
CARRINGTON: Not much.
GERTLER: But he's just a disgusting pervert.
CARRINGTON: You always have to put up with something.
   (*Despite the incongruity of this remark, she makes it with an
   odd dignity. She pulls away from him, walks down the stairs,
   crosses the crowded hallway, quietly and deliberately takes*
   LYTTON's *hand and leads him away.*)

EXT. TOW-PATH. NIGHT
*Moonlit night. A small front garden leads on to a tow-path alongside
the Thames, in the shadow of Hammersmith Bridge. The pavements
are shiny with rain.* LYTTON *walks arm in arm with* CARRINGTON
along the tow-path.
LYTTON: It's very bright tonight, do you think there'll be a raid?
   (*Suddenly* GERTLER *comes hurtling out of the house, grabs*
   LYTTON's *sleeve, spins him round and smashes both fists into his
   face.* LYTTON *goes down like a ninepin.* GERTLER *hurls himself
   full length on top of him and gets hold of handfuls of his hair.*)
GERTLER: Have you managed it yet? Have you?
   (GUESTS *begin to drag him off and away from* LYTTON. *He
   struggles violently.* LYTTON *scrambles to his feet.*
   BELL *and* MARY *dust him down and lead him away.*

Meanwhile, another three GUESTS *restrain* GERTLER *with difficulty*.)
I'll kill him!
(LYTTON *giggles nervously*.)
LYTTON: That was all rather thrilling. (*As he's led away, his voice rises again, a trifle hysterically*.) Anything more cinematographic could scarcely be imagined.
(GERTLER *is being led back towards the house, shouting incoherently;* LYTTON *is being taken off down the tow-path, giggling; alone now, by the river, rooted to the spot, frightened, looking first one way and then the other, is* CARRINGTON.)

FADE

CAPTION ON BLACK SCREEN

THREE
PARTRIDGE 1918–1921

CARRINGTON: (*Voiceover*) Rex Partridge, the young man I was telling you about, is coming down to see us on Friday.

EXT. THE MILL HOUSE. DAY

PARTRIDGE, *twenty-three, tall, powerfully built, blond, blue-eyed and pink-cheeked, wearing a Major's uniform, cycles down the slope towards the front door of the Mill House, singing, at maximum volume, 'la Donna e Mobile'.*

CARRINGTON: (*Voiceover*) After the war he plans to sail a
    schooner to the Mediterranean islands and trade in wine
    and dress like a brigand.
    (PARTRIDGE *lets his bicycle drop and raps smartly at the door.*)

INT. DINING ROOM. DAY

LYTTON*'s chair is pulled back from the table, so that his face is in shadow.*

  He is staring silently and greedily at PARTRIDGE, *who at the moment is demolishing an apple.* CARRINGTON *sits opposite him, her expression somewhat agitated. Remains of lunch on the table.*

CARRINGTON: You mean that you enjoy it?
PARTRIDGE: Well, no, it's not that I enjoy it, of course not, but it
    does seem a good deal more real over there. And it's a
    relief to get out of range of all those Bolsheviks and
    malingerers who spend all their time complaining about
    subjects they don't know the first thing about.
    (*Silence.* CARRINGTON *shoots a quick look at* LYTTON *and sees
    he has no intention of saying anything.*)
CARRINGTON: If you mean conscientious objectors . . .
PARTRIDGE: I do. That's exactly what I mean. Only I call them
    skulkers.
CARRINGTON: A lot of them are prepared to suffer for their
    beliefs, you know. Bertie Russell's in jail.
PARTRIDGE: Best place for him, I daresay. Anyway, he's better
    off there than in the trenches, isn't he?
CARRINGTON: That's not the point . . .
PARTRIDGE: 'Course it is.
CARRINGTON: What are you supposed to do if you're a pacifist,
    what, what would you suggest?
PARTRIDGE: What would I suggest?
CARRINGTON: Yes.
PARTRIDGE: I'd suggest they were put up against a wall and
    shot, that's what I'd suggest.

(*Silence.* CARRINGTON *is profoundly shocked.* LYTTON *watches, silent.*)

INT. BATHROOM. NIGHT
LYTTON *is sitting up in his bath to allow* CARRINGTON *to sponge his back. Absorbed and tender, she rinses off the soap.*
CARRINGTON: I'm so sorry.
    (LYTTON *looks up, surprised.*)
LYTTON: What for?
CARRINGTON: I thought you'd like him.
LYTTON: What do you mean?
CARRINGTON: I'm sorry he was so awful.
    (LYTTON *looks at her a moment, genuinely puzzled.*)
LYTTON: But I thought he was wonderful.

EXT. GARDEN OF THE MILL HOUSE. DAY
Blazing sun. LYTTON *lies in the shade wearing a white Brahminical robe. He's surrounded by a sea of newspapers.* CARRINGTON *sits nearby in the sun, sketching the mill-race.*
LYTTON: (*Flourishing* The Times) 'Thanks to the brilliancy of his style, *Eminent Victorians* is a fascinating book.' I suppose this is what must be meant by the phrase 'to wake up famous'. Chatto's say the book is selling so well, they've been forced to consider a reprint, that's bad luck, isn't it?
    (CARRINGTON *smiles at him; he reaches for one of the newspapers.*)
I can't claim it was my intention to demolish Victorian values once and for all: but if that's what I've done, I'm not in the least sorry.

INT. LYTTON'S BEDROOM IN THE MILL HOUSE. NIGHT
LYTTON *and* CARRINGTON *lie in bed in each other's arms. She is playing with his beard, curling it round her fingers. An atmosphere of profound contentment.*
LYTTON: It seems I'm in distinct danger of becoming a man of means.
    (*On the bed is a copy of the* Times Literary Supplement, *which he indicates.*)
Terrible review by Gosse. I can't tell you what a relief it is

to be denounced at last. It hasn't been easy, remaining calm in the face of hysterical praise from the *Daily Telegraph*.

(CARRINGTON *pulls his face towards her and kisses his forehead.*)

The curse of it all is, I can't see how to get out of writing another book, can you?

(*She kisses him again.*)

INT. SITTING ROOM IN THE MILL HOUSE. DAY

CARRINGTON *brings* LYTTON *a cup of tea and a scone, sets them down on his desk. He takes a sip of tea. She stands, looking down at him.*

LYTTON: I don't know why you're so good to me, it's a constant mystery.

(CARRINGTON *picks up a penwiper from Lytton's desk. It's made of red and blue felt with ragged edges, and on it, embroidered in green, are the words 'USE ME'.*)

CARRINGTON: That's how I feel, Lytton. You must always remember that. I'm your penwiper.

INT. FLAT IN THE ADELPHI. NIGHT

Armistice Day. The flat is packed with celebrating people. Most of the GUESTS *are very formally dressed, but the atmosphere is riotous, even slightly hysterical. Music and dancing. Seated at a table to one side are* LYTTON *and* CARRINGTON, OTTOLINE *and* PARTRIDGE. *The latter is still in uniform, while the others form a striking contrast to the tailcoats and ball gowns.* OTTOLINE *is in her most spectacular outfit, her hair vivid with henna.*

LYTTON: I know it was an obscene and ridiculous war, but I suppose it's quite convenient to have won.

OTTOLINE: Now we shall see real progress, Lytton. We are on the threshold of a Golden Age!

(LYTTON *smiles, a touch cynically, then is suddenly caught up in the spirit of the occasion.*)

LYTTON: Do you know, Ottoline, given the circumstances, I really think we ought to dance.

OTTOLINE: Very well.

(*They take the floor.* LYTTON *jigs amiably up and down,*

36

completely out of time with the music; OTTOLINE's *methods are more dramatic. They make a spectacularly peculiar couple.* CARRINGTON *and* RALPH *join them on the dance floor. She is watching* LYTTON *intently.*)

CARRINGTON: I wish he'd worn his pullover.

PARTRIDGE: I must say, to look at him, you wouldn't think he could have written that book.

CARRINGTON: Why not?

PARTRIDGE: I read it the other day, couldn't see what all the fuss was about.

(CARRINGTON *frowns indignantly at him.*)

LYTTON: (*Voiceover, reading from* The Duchess of Malfi)
Cardinal: I'll leave you.
Ferdinand: Nay, I have done.
I am confident, had I been damned in Hell,
And should have heard of this, it would have put me
Into a cold sweat.

INT. SITTING-ROOM IN THE MILL HOUSE. EVENING

LYTTON: In, in, I'll go sleep:
Till I know who leaps my sister, I'll not stir.
That known, I'll find scorpions to string my whips,
And fix her in a general eclipse.
Exeunt.

(LYTTON, CARRINGTON *and* PARTRIDGE: LYTTON *lays the book aside.*)
I've been meaning to tell you: I can't say I really approve of Rex.

PARTRIDGE: What do you mean?

LYTTON: As a name.

PARTRIDGE: It's not my real name.

(LYTTON *looks at him, waiting.*)
My real name is Reginald.

LYTTON: Ah.

(*Silence.*)
Myself, I'm very much in favour of Ralph.

(*He pronounces it 'Rafe'.* PARTRIDGE *looks at him, frowning.*)

LYTTON: Ralph Partridge. Ralph Partridge. It sounds very well, don't you agree? Ralph.

37

EXT. GARDEN OF THE MILL HOUSE. DAY

PARTRIDGE *reclines, naked, smiling, in the long grass in a corner of the garden by the mill-race.*

CARRINGTON *is drawing him, concentrating, her tongue slightly protruding.*

PARTRIDGE: What's the matter?

(*She sighs, shakes her head, tears up the sketch.*)

CARRINGTON: I don't know. I seem to be in rather a flux.

(PARTRIDGE *smiles knowingly.*)

EXT. ST. EDMUND HALL BOAT HOUSE, OXFORD. DAY

LYTTON *sits alone on a canvas chair, patiently staring out at the river. Eventually, a boat appears.* PARTRIDGE *is one of the eight. He rows powerfully and rhythmically.*

LYTTON: (*Voiceover*) It's really not fair. Why aren't I a rowing blue, with eyes to match?

(LYTTON *risks a little wave: as the boat speeds by,* PARTRIDGE *flashes a broad grin at him.*)

CARRINGTON: (*Voiceover*) That's all very well, but his conversation is so dull. He's like some Norwegian dentist.

EXT. RIVER IN CORNWALL. DAY

A pool beside a small waterfall. PARTRIDGE *and* CARRINGTON *are swimming naked. He swims towards her as she floats on her back. She shrieks as he capsizes her.*

LYTTON: (*Voiceover*) I suppose your privileges give you the right to judge.

INT. CARRINGTON'S BEDROOM IN THE MILL HOUSE. NIGHT

LYTTON *is in bed with* CARRINGTON.

LYTTON: I don't know what the world is coming to. Ladies in love with buggers and buggers in love with womanizers – and what with the price of coal . . .

(CARRINGTON *laughs.*)

Do you think your Major would stay more often if you had a more comfortable bed?

CARRINGTON: The bed's all right.

LYTTON: Let me put it another way: I wish he would stay more often.

MIX TO

INT. CARRINGTON'S BEDROOM. NIGHT
CARRINGTON *and* PARTRIDGE *lie entwined in a huge new four-poster bed, brilliantly decorated by* CARRINGTON.
PARTRIDGE: When you go up to London . . .
CARRINGTON: Mm.
PARTRIDGE: Who do you see?
CARRINGTON: Nobody you know.
PARTRIDGE: Yes, but who?
     (*Silence.*)
CARRINGTON: I like to keep a bit of privacy in my life, you
     know. And if you're going to cross-examine me all the
     time, that seems very much like jealousy, and I don't
     believe in that.
PARTRIDGE: Well, if you don't believe in it, why should you
     mind telling me who you see when you go to London?
     (*His tone is light, but* CARRINGTON *isn't pleased. She turns
     away from him.*)

EXT. GARDEN OF THE MILL HOUSE. DAY
Blazing summer's day. PARTRIDGE, *wearing only a dirty pair of
white shorts, is feeding the ducks in the mill-race.*
     LYTTON, *in dark suit and panama hat, sits in a deckchair, a book
open on his knee, watching him.* CARRINGTON *is watering the flower-
bed.*
LYTTON: Yes, but will I like him?
PARTRIDGE: Gerald? I don't see why not. Long as you don't
     frighten him.
LYTTON: I can't imagine what you mean.
PARTRIDGE: Well, he's shy. I used to take him to the brothel in
     Amiens . . .

EXT. THE MILL HOUSE. DAY
GERALD BRENAN *advances slowly down the path towards the door
which opens directly to the sitting-room. He's twenty-five, compact,
handsome and has a small moustache. His eyes are large and
dreamy. His clothes – an open greyish shirt, an ancient sports jacket
and grey flannels – are strikingly shabby.*
PARTRIDGE: (*Voiceover*) . . . but he always used to wait
     downstairs or slope off to look at the cathedral.

39

(BRENAN *reaches the front door, hesitates and lifts a hand to knock. As he does so, he becomes aware that the leather patch on his elbow is flapping loose. He starts to adjust this, when the top half of the door is suddenly flung open by* CARRINGTON, *startling him considerably. She's wearing a blue dress.*)

CARRINGTON: You must be Gerald Brenan.

BRENAN: Miss Carrington?

CARRINGTON: Carrington.

BRENAN: Rex . . . that's to say, Ralph . . . tells me you're a Bolshevik.

CARRINGTON: He tells me you're an idealist.

    (*They smile. They like each other.*)

INT. DINING ROOM. DAY

The remains of lunch on the table. BRENAN *is holding an apple, speaking excitedly.* CARRINGTON *is next to him,* PARTRIDGE *opposite and* LYTTON *at the head of the table, glaring at* BRENAN.

BRENAN: I'm going to look for a house in Spain.

LYTTON: Why?

BRENAN: To educate myself.

LYTTON: Unlikely reason.

BRENAN: I'm too old to go to university now and I have to do something to repair my ignorance. So I'm eloping with two thousand books.

LYTTON: Why Spain?

BRENAN: Because it's hot and cheap.

LYTTON: True.

BRENAN: And the women are beautiful.

LYTTON: Sounds worse and worse.

    (BRENAN *begins, carefully and fastidiously, to peel his apple. Next to him,* CARRINGTON *is peeling an apple in precisely the same way.* PARTRIDGE *watches them for a moment. Then he reaches for an apple and removes almost half of it with a mighty bite.*)

EXT. WOODS NEAR TIDMARSH. DAY

PARTRIDGE, *stripped to the waist, and* CARRINGTON *manage to coax and negotiate* LYTTON *along a log, fallen across a narrow stream.*

BRENAN *brings up the rear. Once over the stream,* LYTTON *strides on ahead with* PARTRIDGE, *a hand on his shoulder, while* BRENAN *and* CARRINGTON *follow at a more leisurely pace, some yards behind.*

BRENAN: You mustn't believe everything Ralph tells you about me.

CARRINGTON: Why do you say that?

BRENAN: He invents everyone he meets. You must have noticed. He gives them a character and a set of opinions so he can argue with them.

(CARRINGTON *looks at him, impressed by this insight.*)

CARRINGTON: I suppose you're right.

(*Silence. They walk on.*)

BRENAN: I don't mean to attack Ralph. He's my closest friend. But he lives entirely by his instincts and I can't do that. I wish I could.

CARRINGTON: Isn't going off to live in Spain following your instincts?

BRENAN: Not really. I'd say it was very calculated. It has to be.

CARRINGTON: You mean, money?

BRENAN: I'm told you can rent a house there for five pounds a year.

(*They walk on a little further.*)

CARRINGTON: Whereabouts in Spain are you going?

BRENAN: No idea.

(CARRINGTON *smiles and* BRENAN *counters defensively.*)

I have a map.

(CARRINGTON *laughs: they walk on.*)

CARRINGTON: Well, I hope you'll write to me.

BRENAN: Of course, I'll write to both of you.

CARRINGTON: Separately.

(BRENAN *smiles back, somewhat uncertain.*)

INT. SITTING-ROOM IN THE MILL HOUSE. EVENING

LYTTON *sits in his armchair, reading Shakespeare.* CARRINGTON *is writing a letter, scribbling away at great speed. On the old horn gramophone, hissing and scratching is Schubert's Quintet. Late sun pours into the room.* CARRINGTON *looks up.*

CARRINGTON: How d'you spell intangible?

(LYTTON *spells it for her.* CARRINGTON *looks at what she's written, frowning.*)
Oh, well, never mind.

INT./EXT. CARRINGTON'S BEDROOM IN THE MILL HOUSE. DAY
CARRINGTON *stands at her window, staring wistfully out across the fields.* LYTTON *is sitting on a deck-chair reading in the shade.*

INT. SITTING-ROOM IN THE MILL HOUSE. EVENING
LYTTON *moves around the room, clearly agitated and upset.*
PARTRIDGE *watches him, waiting. The sound of distant thunder.*
LYTTON: Won't you be just some glorified typesetter?
PARTRIDGE: No. And that's not really the point, is it?
LYTTON: Oh, what is the point?
PARTRIDGE: The point is, I shall have to live in London. And I want Carrington to come with me.
LYTTON: Oh. I see.
PARTRIDGE: We'll come back here every weekend. And the servants will look after you during the week.
LYTTON: It's not the same: I shall miss you terribly.
PARTRIDGE: It won't be so very different. All your gallivanting about, you know yourself you're only here about half the time, except when you're working, and then it'll be an advantage to be on your own.
(*Silence.* LYTTON *reflects, morosely.*)
LYTTON: Suppose she doesn't agree.
PARTRIDGE: Then I think it would be best for me to make a complete break.
(LYTTON *is shocked. He stares for a moment at the dominating figure of* PARTRIDGE.)
LYTTON: My darling. I don't think I could face that.

INT. CARRINGTON'S BEDROOM. NIGHT
CARRINGTON *and* PARTRIDGE *are undressing, ready for bed. A few seconds' heavy silence.*
CARRINGTON: Why do you think I moved away from London in the first place? I hate London.
PARTRIDGE: That's rather a selfish attitude.
CARRINGTON: I can't just . . . abandon Lytton.

PARTRIDGE: I think you'll find he doesn't quite see it in that
light.
(CARRINGTON *stops in the act of taking off her shoe and looks at*
PARTRIDGE, *real fear in her eyes.*)
CARRINGTON: What do you mean?

INT. CARRINGTON'S BEDROOM. NIGHT
Semi-darkness. LYTTON, CARRINGTON *and* PARTRIDGE *are all in the*
four-poster bed, PARTRIDGE *in the middle.* CARRINGTON *is asleep.*
LYTTON *is stroking* PARTRIDGE's *hair, whispering to him.*
LYTTON: There are times when I feel like a character in a farce
by Molière: *Le Bougre Marié.* (*He snuggles closer to*
PARTRIDGE.) I do wish you weren't quite so single-minded,
dearest. I mean, I have tried, I can't help it, women's
bodies, I find, somehow, subtly offensive. Or reproachful,
would it be? Something.
(*He leans forward to nibble at* PARTRIDGE's *ear.* PARTRIDGE's
expression is good-natured but by no means responsive.)

EXT. BERKSHIRE DOWNS. DAY
Damp autumn landscape. PARTRIDGE *and* CARRINGTON *stride*
through the bracken.

43

PARTRIDGE: Lytton said a strange thing last night.
CARRINGTON: Oh, yes, what?
PARTRIDGE: He told me he thought women's bodies were disgusting.
(CARRINGTON *looks at him, shocked, as if she's just been slapped in the face.*)

INT. LYTTON'S BEDROOM IN THE MILL HOUSE. EVENING
LYTTON *is squeezing shut an old leather suitcase. Another lies on the floor, already packed. A knock at the door. He looks up, lets go the lid of the suitcase.*
CARRINGTON: (*Off-screen*) Can I come in?
LYTTON: Of course.
(*The door swings open and* CARRINGTON *appears, both hands behind her back.* LYTTON *smiles at her, mystified.*)
CARRINGTON: Two indispensable items you've forgotten. (*She brings one hand from behind her back and flourishes a pair of binoculars.*) These. Very handy for boy-watching in Italy. (*LYTTON takes them, smiling. Then she brings out her other hand, in which she's holding the light-brown air cushion, limp and uninflated.*)
And.

(LYTTON *takes it.*)

LYTTON: You are wonderful. You think of everything. I shall give you a kiss.

(*He does so.* CARRINGTON *smiles, although there is panic in her eyes. He notices.*)

CARRINGTON: What am I going to do, Lytton?

LYTTON: He's very determined, my dear. He tells me if you don't marry him he's resolved to go and live abroad.

CARRINGTON: If only I wasn't so plural. Especially when people seem to want me so . . . conclusively.

LYTTON: I'm sure you'll do the right thing.

(*His face is expressionless. She looks at him, frightened.*)

INT. SITTING-ROOM OF PARTRIDGE'S FLAT. EVENING

CARRINGTON *and* PARTRIDGE *are in the middle of an argument.*

CARRINGTON: I can't see what possible difference getting married would make.

PARTRIDGE: A great deal of difference.

CARRINGTON: It's just a piece of paper.

PARTRIDGE: For one thing, think how much easier it would be travelling abroad . . . and . . . and . . .

CARRINGTON: And what?

(PARTRIDGE *leaps to his feet, enraged by the coldness in* CARRINGTON'*s voice.*)

PARTRIDGE: Well, if that's the way you feel, there's only one thing for it. (*He pauses, expecting a question which doesn't come.*) I shall go to Bolivia.

CARRINGTON: What?

PARTRIDGE: A man I know in Oxford wants me to run a sheep farm in Bolivia.

(CARRINGTON *looks at him a moment, then bursts out laughing.*) I'm quite serious! I can't go on like this!

CARRINGTON: Don't be ridiculous.

PARTRIDGE: I will not be treated like a child! (*He strides out of the room, slamming the door.*)

INT. WORKMEN'S CAFE. DAY

CARRINGTON *and* PARTRIDGE *face each other across the cheap wooden table. Congealing, untouched fried eggs and bread and butter*

45

in front of PARTRIDGE. *A large china mug of milky tea in front of*
CARRINGTON. PARTRIDGE *looks grey and ill;* CARRINGTON
exhausted, cornered.

PARTRIDGE: If I go, he won't let you live with him any more,
you know that, don't you?

CARRINGTON: He's never said that.

PARTRIDGE: I don't think he wants to see you again when he
gets back from Italy.
(CARRINGTON *is dumbfounded.*)

INT. LYTTON'S BEDROOM IN THE MILL HOUSE. DAY
CARRINGTON *stands beneath the Adam mural.*

CARRINGTON: (*Voiceover*) My dearest Lytton. There is a great
deal to say and I feel very incompetent to write it today.

INT. PRIVATE APARTMENT AT I TATTI, FLORENCE. DAY
LYTTON *sits, marooned in a vast, palatially-furnished room, reading
a letter.*

CARRINGTON: (*Voiceover*) You see, I knew there was nothing
really to hope for from you, well, ever since the beginning.

INT./EXT. CARRINGTON'S BEDROOM IN THE MILL HOUSE. DAY
CARRINGTON *stands at her window, as before, looking out across the
fields. This time,* LYTTON*'s deckchair beneath the tree is empty.*

INT. BATHROOM IN THE MILL HOUSE. DAY
CARRINGTON *slips into the bathroom, crosses to the bath, picks up
Lytton's sponge and smells it.*

CARRINGTON: (*Voiceover*) All these years I have known all along
that my life with you was limited. Lytton, you are the only
person who I have ever had an all-absorbing passion for. I
shall never have another. I couldn't now. I had one of the
most self-abasing loves that a person can have.

INT. PARTRIDGE'S FLAT IN GORDON SQUARE. DAY
CARRINGTON *stands at the window, craning to look at the square
below.*

CARRINGTON: (*Voiceover*) It's too much of a strain to be quite
alone here waiting to see you . . .

EXT. GORDON SQUARE. DAY
LYTTON's *panama hat appears, bobbing up and down above the hedge on the other side of the square.*
CARRINGTON: (*Voiceover*) . . . or craning my nose and eyes out of the top window at 44, Gordon Square to see if you were coming down the street.

INT. PARTRIDGE'S FLAT. DAY
CARRINGTON *reacts, delighted to see* LYTTON *approaching.*

INT. CARRINGTON'S BEDROOM IN THE MILL HOUSE. NIGHT
PARTRIDGE *is making love to* CARRINGTON. *She looks up at the ceiling, virtually expressionless.*
CARRINGTON: (*Voiceover*) Ralph said you were nervous lest I'd feel I had some sort of claim on you and that all your friends wondered how you could have stood me so long, as I didn't understand a word of literature.

INT. CARRINGTON'S BEDROOM. NIGHT
Later. PARTRIDGE *is heavily asleep,* CARRINGTON *silently weeps.*
CARRINGTON: (*Voiceover*) That was wrong. For nobody, I think, could have loved the Ballades, Donne, and Macaulay's Essays, and, best of all, Lytton's Essays, as much as I.

EXT. GARDEN IN THE MILL HOUSE. DAY
CARRINGTON *carries a cup of tea and some buttered toast across to* LYTTON's *table, set up under a tree, facing the house. He looks up in pleasurable anticipation.*
CARRINGTON: (*Voiceover*) You never knew, or never will know, the very big and devastating love I had for you. How I adored every hair, every curl of your beard. Just thinking of you now makes me cry so I can't see this paper.

EXT. TERRACE AND GARDEN AT I TATTI. DAY
LYTTON *sits at a long wooden table on the terrace outside the villa; he puts aside* CARRINGTON's *letter and takes up his pen.*
CARRINGTON: (*Voiceover*) Once you said to me, that Wednesday afternoon in the sitting-room, you loved me as a friend. Could you tell it to me again? Yours, Carrington.

(*Close on* LYTTON: *tears glisten in his eyes. He begins to write.*)
LYTTON: (*Voiceover*) My dearest and best . . . (*He breaks off and looks up, reflecting.*)
(*Long shot:* LYTTON *is seated on the terrace, in the lea of the villa.*)
(*Voiceover*) Do you know how difficult I find it to express my feelings either in letters or talk?

INT. ST. PANCRAS REGISTRY OFFICE. DAY
PARTRIDGE *and* CARRINGTON *stand in front of the registrar.*
PARTRIDGE *pushes a narrow, plain gold ring onto* CARRINGTON'S *finger. She looks lost and unhappy.*
LYTTON: (*Voiceover*) . . . do you really want me to tell you that I love you as a friend? But of course that is absurd and you do know very well that I love you as something more than a friend, you angelic creature, whose goodness to me has made me happy for years. Your letter made me cry, I feel a poor old miserable creature.

INT. GRAND STAIRCASE TO THE ST. PANCRAS REGISTRY OFFICE. DAY
CARRINGTON *moves slowly down the stairs, slumped on* PARTRIDGE'S *arm.*
LYTTON: (*Voiceover*) If there was a chance that your decision meant that I should somehow or other lose you, I don't think I could bear it. You and Ralph and our life at Tidmarsh are what I care for most in the world.

EXT. SIDE CANAL IN VENICE. DAY
The handsome young GONDOLIER *beams at* LYTTON, *who sits sideways on in the small upright armchair.* CARRINGTON *and* PARTRIDGE *are side-by-side on the banquette;* PARTRIDGE'S *arm is loosely draped around* CARRINGTON'S *shoulders.*
LYTTON: Well, I think I shall spend all my honeymoons here.
(*His eye falls on* CARRINGTON'S *left hand.*) Shouldn't you be wearing a ring?
CARRINGTON: I lost it. Somewhere in the Italian Alps.
(*She looks at* LYTTON, *sitting opposite, expansive and contented.*) Do you ever get terrified of dying?
(*Silence, except for the splash of the oar. Then the* GONDOLIER

utters a melancholy cry and steers the gondola round a blind corner.)

FADE

CAPTION ON BLACK SCREEN

FOUR
BRENAN 1921–1923

On sound: the buzz and hum of an English summer's day.

EXT. WHITE HORSE HILL. UFFINGTON. DAY
BRENAN *lies on a rug, propping himself up on one elbow, close to a chalk indentation which forms part of the giant white horse etched into the hillside. Above him,* CARRINGTON *sketches: him and the vast tract of countryside spread out below. Remains of a picnic nearby. Two bicycles lie on the ground.* CARRINGTON *puts down her sketchpad and moves down the hill to join* BRENAN.
CARRINGTON: When you've been married as long as six weeks, you've no idea how pleasant it is to get away on your own.

(BRENAN *smiles uncertainly, hesitates before speaking.*)
BRENAN: I sometimes wish I'd met you before Ralph did.
CARRINGTON: Yes.
BRENAN: I don't suppose I'd have made much impression on
you.
(*Instead of answering,* CARRINGTON *leans forward and kisses
him on the lips.* BRENAN*'s eyes register surprise and a touch of
alarm. Then he submits. Long kiss. Then* CARRINGTON *breaks
away and smiles down at him. A long silence.* BRENAN *sits,
looking at her, completely bewildered.*)

INT. SITTING-ROOM IN THE MILL HOUSE. EVENING
Sunset. BRENAN *sits in an armchair, reading.* CARRINGTON *is
moving round the room, putting flowers in vases and arranging
them. As she finishes doing this,* BRENAN *looks up from his book.*
CARRINGTON *begins to cross the room, stops for a moment in front of
a window, through which the evening sun streams in.* BRENAN *is
watching her. His mouth is open and a look, almost of pained
amazement, comes into his eyes.* CARRINGTON *notices.*
CARRINGTON: What's the matter?
BRENAN: I don't know . . .
(*He stops. They look at each other, transfixed. Suddenly, the
door bursts open, startling both of them, and* PARTRIDGE
*appears. He's wearing white shorts and a rowing vest and is in
the best of spirits.*)
PARTRIDGE: You know something, Gerald, you're mad. Why
d'you have to go back to Spain so soon ? Why don't you
come and join us on holiday?
(*Silence.* BRENAN *looks as if he's in pain.*)
BRENAN: No, I couldn't.

EXT. DERELICT BARN. DAY
CARRINGTON *is painting a portrait of* BRENAN, *concentrating
intently, when* PARTRIDGE *appears, rod in hand.*
PARTRIDGE: Ready?
CARRINGTON: This is going very well, do you mind awfully?
PARTRIDGE: Not at all. (*He waves his fishing rod as he leaves.*)

EXT. RIVERBANK. DAY
PARTRIDGE *sits motionless on the banks of the river, fishing. He reaches absently towards a newspaper parcel, fumbles in it for a moment, fetches out a hard-boiled egg, which he cracks and peels dexterously with one hand, and starts to eat, never allowing his concentration to wander. The camera rises, pulling away from this scene to a high angle, to reveal, concealed from* PARTRIDGE *by a wall, the abandoned easel standing outside the rough stone barn.*

INT. DERELICT BARN. DAY
CARRINGTON *and* BRENAN *lie entwined in the hayloft, kissing passionately. Finally, reluctantly, he pulls away from her.*
BRENAN: I must tell Ralph.
CARRINGTON: What?
BRENAN: I must. I can't bear this deceit. After all, he is one of
    my oldest friends. I think I ought to go and tell him I love
    you, that he has nothing to worry about, that it's just like
    brother and sister . . .
    (*He breaks off.* CARRINGTON *is staring at him in some anxiety.*)
CARRINGTON: I shouldn't.
BRENAN: Why not?
CARRINGTON: You'd upset him.

BRENAN: But surely . . .

CARRINGTON: You would, really you would. He's such a dear, it wouldn't be fair. I feel shittish enough about it as it is.
(*She reaches out and puts her hands on his cheeks, draws him down to her. They kiss.*)

BRENAN: I want you to come back to Spain with me. Now. Today. And live with me.

CARRINGTON: I can't, Gerald.

BRENAN: Why not?
(CARRINGTON *doesn't answer. Instead, she reaches for him and glues her mouth to his.*)
I feel as if I'm drowning.

EXT. COUNTRY ROAD NEAR WATENDLATH FARM. DAY
Sunny day. PARTRIDGE *strides along the road, humming a folk-song.* BRENAN, *with his rucksack, and* CARRINGTON *trail along behind, looking strained and tense, groping surreptitiously for one another's hand. They come to a fork in the road.* PARTRIDGE *stops.*

PARTRIDGE: Well, old chap, I think this is the parting of the ways.

BRENAN: Yes.
(*Silence. Then* BRENAN *and* PARTRIDGE *shake hands.*)

PARTRIDGE: Take care of yourself.

BRENAN: I will.
(*He stretches out his hand to* CARRINGTON, *who takes it.*)

PARTRIDGE: Oh, I think the lady and gentleman might be permitted a kiss, don't you?
(BRENAN *leans forward and pecks at* CARRINGTON*'s cheek. Then he turns on his heel and hurries away.* PARTRIDGE *and* CARRINGTON *stand, watching him go. She looks close to tears. Abruptly, she turns away and sets off down the other fork. Presently,* PARTRIDGE *catches her up.*)
I really don't understand you, a bit of effort.

CARRINGTON: What do you mean?

PARTRIDGE: Well, if you'd just tried to persuade him, I'm sure he'd have stayed another couple of days.

INT./EXT. CARRINGTON'S BEDROOM IN THE MILL HOUSE. EVENING
CARRINGTON *is working on the Brenan portrait.* LYTTON *opens the door and hovers in the doorway.*

LYTTON: Do you know if Ralph's coming back this evening?
> (*There's just the faintest hint of disappointment in his voice, which* CARRINGTON *registers.*)

CARRINGTON: He said he had some work to do in London.
> (LYTTON *moves into the room and shuts the door.*)
>
> I don't know who it is, Lytton.
> (LYTTON *walks towards* CARRINGTON, *looking at Brenan's portrait.*)
>
> I've had three letters already this week.
> (LYTTON *looks at her shrewdly.*)
>
> I miss him terribly.

LYTTON: When is he coming back to England?

CARRINGTON: He says he can't afford the fare.
> (LYTTON *considers this carefully for some time.*)

EXT. DOWNS ABOVE TIDMARSH. DAY
BRENAN strides across the rolling hills. There's a rucksack on his back and a rolled up rug across his shoulders.

INT. CARRINGTON'S BEDROOM. DAY
CARRINGTON and BRENAN are on their knees unrolling a handsome Spanish rug.

CARRINGTON: It's lovely, Gerald, I shall always treasure it.
> (*Suddenly, they're locked in a violent embrace, sprawling on the rug. Eventually,* BRENAN *manages to extricate himself and pulls back.* CARRINGTON *grabs at his wrist.*)
>
> Look, this is silly. Ralph has mistresses, you know, I'm sure he's with one of them now; so I can't see the sense in it.
> (*She pulls* BRENAN *towards her and they kiss; then, once again, they're sprawling on the rug.* BRENAN *starts to unbutton her dress.*)

INT. SITTING-ROOM IN THE MILLHOUSE. DAY
LYTTON is reading Gibbon. He looks up from the book at the sound of CARRINGTON, *crying out with pleasure.*

INT. CARRINGTON'S BEDROOM. DAY
CARRINGTON lies in BRENAN's *arms; he looks down at her tenderly.*

BRENAN: Now will you come back to Spain with me?

54

(CARRINGTON *shakes her head gravely.*)
CARRINGTON: You mustn't spoil things, Gerald.
BRENAN: You want to stay in England with Ralph . . .
CARRINGTON: No. Not with Ralph. With Lytton.

EXT. THE MILL HOUSE. NIGHT
PARTRIDGE *stands in the garden, clutching an almost empty whisky
bottle which he now proceeds to drain.*
PARTRIDGE: Carrington!
    (*A light goes on upstairs.* PARTRIDGE *throws the whisky bottle
    against the wall, shattering it.*)

INT. LYTTON'S BEDROOM. NIGHT
LYTTON, *wakes in alarm. As* PARTRIDGE'*s voice rings out again,*
LYTTON *decides to stay where he is and let matters take their course.*

EXT. THE MILL HOUSE. NIGHT
PARTRIDGE *is lurching towards the front door, when it opens.*
CARRINGTON *stands in the doorway, blinking out into the night.*
PARTRIDGE: Where's Brenan?
CARRINGTON: He's not here.
PARTRIDGE: I said where is he?
CARRINGTON: I told you. He's not here.
PARTRIDGE: I'll kill him!
CARRINGTON: Has somebody told you something? Who?
PARTRIDGE: None of your business. Out of the way!
CARRINGTON: He's gone to stay with his parents.
PARTRIDGE: Will you get out of the way! I'm going to pull his
    arms off. (*He storms past her and vanishes into the house.*)

INT. STAIRCASE AND LANDING. NIGHT
CARRINGTON *runs after* PARTRIDGE *as he bounds upstairs.*

INT. CARRINGTON'S BEDROOM. NIGHT
PARTRIDGE *bursts into the room. It's empty. As* CARRINGTON
*appears in the doorway, so he's striding over to look under the four-
poster bed.*
PARTRIDGE: Where is he?

INT. BRENAN'S BASEMENT ROOM IN LONDON. DAY
Grey day, poor light. The flat is poor and shabby; not much of anything. PARTRIDGE *and* BRENAN *sit, not looking at each other. They both look terrible,* PARTRIDGE *hung-over and unshaven,* BRENAN *miserable and uncomfortable.*
   Heavy silence.
PARTRIDGE: So, you were in love with her?
BRENAN: Yes.
PARTRIDGE: And you're trying to tell me that you haven't been fucking her, do you expect me to believe that?
BRENAN: Yes.
PARTRIDGE: I know you're pretty feeble, Gerald, but what exactly is the meaning of this heroic self-restraint?
BRENAN: I was always very aware that you're my friend and she's my wife, I mean, your wife.
   (*Silence.*)
PARTRIDGE: All right, let's go through this step by step, shall we? Now presumably you kissed her. I mean you must have kissed her.
BRENAN: I suppose so, yes.
PARTRIDGE: And did you, for example . . . did you ever put your hand down the front of her dress?
BRENAN: No, I don't think so.
PARTRIDGE: You don't think so. I'm asking you if you ever touched her tits?
BRENAN: No. (*He shakes his head wearily.*) What's the point of all this?
PARTRIDGE: The point is, the point of it is, this is all important information because I have to decide whether I ever want to see either of you again, that's the point of it.
   (*Silence.*)
   Another thing, you realize I can't possibly allow you to see or communicate with her ever again.

INT. DINING-ROOM IN THE MILL HOUSE. DAY
CARRINGTON *and* BRENAN *sit facing each other across the dining-room table.* LYTTON *sits at the head of the table, chewing gravely. Funereal atmosphere.* BRENAN*'s hands are shaking, he seems to be in a state of shock.*

BRENAN: Having to lie to him, that's what I couldn't bear.

LYTTON: We know that, Gerald, but you must understand it was essential.

BRENAN: I suppose so, I don't know . . .

LYTTON: I don't approve of jealousy any more than you do, but no doubt if one's afflicted with it, there's very little one can do about it.

BRENAN: Yes, but he's so irrational . . .

LYTTON: We must proceed with extreme caution. Let me see what I can do.

EXT. MILL HOUSE. DAY

The chrome grille of a gleaming four-seater 1922 Morris Oxford reflects a departing taxi and an approaching PARTRIDGE. *He looks grey and exhausted. He hesitates in front of the car and looks up, puzzled, as* LYTTON *joins him.*

PARTRIDGE: What's this? Visitors?

(LYTTON *smiles. He's excited.*)

LYTTON: No. It's by way of a present.

PARTRIDGE: Who for?

LYTTON: Well, since neither Carrington nor I drive . . .

INT./EXT. UPSTAIRS CORRIDOR. DAY

CARRINGTON *at the window, watching.*

Her POV: PARTRIDGE *seizes* LYTTON *and kisses him on both cheeks.*

CARRINGTON *turns wearily away from the window.*

INT. BRENAN'S BASEMENT. EVENING

BRENAN *has obviously done everything in his power to tidy up the very shabby room. There are lilies in a bowl on the dining-table, together with a bottle of wine and a small opened pot of caviar. The fruit bowl on the sideboard is full of fruit.*

He's just starting to lay the table when there's the sound of a key in the lock and CARRINGTON *appears, crossing the small entrance hall.* BRENAN *looks up, surprised, puts down his handful of knives and forks, crosses to* CARRINGTON *and kisses her. She seems a little distant.*

BRENAN: I didn't expect you so early.

(CARRINGTON *notices the preparations and smiles, slightly suspicious.*)

57

CARRINGTON: What's all this? I thought we were going out.
BRENAN: Well, I thought . . .
> (CARRINGTON *picks up the pot of caviar.*)

CARRINGTON: Caviar? Gerald, you can't afford this.
BRENAN: I know.
> (*Silence.* CARRINGTON *is looking at him, puzzled.*)
> I thought I might induce you to stay the night.

CARRINGTON: You know very well how careful we have to be.
BRENAN: Otherwise it seems so sordid.
CARRINGTON: Don't let's quarrel: there isn't time to quarrel.
> (*She sets off across the room in the direction of the bed beneath the skylight, dropping her coat over a sofa on her way. By the bed, she slips off her waistcoat and starts to unbutton her dress.*)
> Come on.
> (BRENAN *advances reluctantly towards her, taking off his jacket en route.*)

EXT. GARDEN OF THE MILL HOUSE. DAY
LYTTON *sits in a deck-chair under the shade of a beach umbrella;* CARRINGTON *sits at his feet in the sun.*
CARRINGTON: He keeps wanting me to go and live with him. Why is he so demanding?
LYTTON: No doubt because he hasn't understood that people in love should never live together. When they do, the invariable result is that they either fall out of love or drive one another insane. Tell him.
CARRINGTON: He wouldn't believe me.
LYTTON: Idealists are nothing but trouble. You can never convince them there's no such thing as the ideal.
CARRINGTON: I can't see what's going to happen. It's frightening me.
LYTTON: Whatever happens, my dear, you're safe here.
> (*She reaches up and takes his hand.*)

INT. GENNARO'S RESTAURANT IN SOHO. EVENING
CARRINGTON *and* BRENAN *have just had dinner. They're drinking coffee.* CARRINGTON *looks at her watch.*
CARRINGTON: I shall have to go in about five minutes.
BRENAN: Aren't you coming back to the flat?

CARRINGTON: I'd rather not tonight, if you don't mind very much.

BRENAN: Then I shall just have to walk the streets until I find a whore.

CARRINGTON: Yes, I expect you will.

(*Hostile silence. Then, all of a sudden,* CARRINGTON *smiles warmly at* BRENAN.)

Shall we have another picnic on The White Horse Hill? A sentimental pilgrimage?

(BRENAN, *taken completely by surprise, can only smile and shake his head.*)

Come at ten on Sunday. I'll meet you there.

EXT. THE MILL HOUSE. DAY

The house stands, beautiful in the soft morning light.

LYTTON: (*Voiceover*) I can't bear the thought of leaving this house.

INT. LYTTON'S BEDROOM IN THE MILL HOUSE. DAY

CARRINGTON *is in bed with* LYTTON.

LYTTON: The orchard, the mill-race, my wonderful room, the garden of Eden.

(*He indicates* CARRINGTON*'s Adam-and-Eve mural.*)

CARRINGTON: Yes, but the rheumatism, Lytton, the lumbago; the rising damp and the falling plaster; the rats in the wainscot.

LYTTON: Very true.

CARRINGTON: I keep thinking I've forgotten something, you know the feeling? (*She shuts her eyes fiercely, and burrows into* LYTTON's *arms.*)

EXT. WHITE HORSE HILL, UFFINGTON. DAY

BRENAN *is alone on the slopes of the hillside, the giant White Horse poised mockingly above him, his bicycle lying some way off in the grass. Cloudy day. He stops to look at his watch, then pivots on his heel, peering in every direction, before continuing to pace up and down. After a while, it comes on to rain.*

FADE

CAPTION ON BLACK SCREEN

FIVE

HAM SPRAY HOUSE 1924–1931

EXT. HAM SPRAY HOUSE IN HUNGERFORD. DAY

The camera approaches a doorway cut into a tall laurel hedge and tracks through it to discover the back of a large, low, interesting house, with irregular windows, unexpectedly placed.

As the camera stops to contemplate the house, CARRINGTON *rides through the gap in the hedge on her white horse, Belle. She dismounts, casually leaving the horse to graze on the large sunken lawn, climbs a few steps, crosses a kind of grass plateau, past a white iron table and chairs and steps into the house.*

INT./EXT. GAMES ROOM. DAY

She's stepped into an empty room with ground sheets, ladders and a trestle. On the trestle are PARTRIDGE, *standing, crowded against the ceiling, screwing in a rose to carry a light fitting; and a very pretty girl of twenty-four,* FRANCES MARSHALL, *who's whitewashing the ceiling. As* CARRINGTON *exchanges greetings with them,* LYTTON *comes into the room from the hallway with* ROGER SENHOUSE, *a handsome student in his early twenties.*

LYTTON: Ralph? Ah, Ralph, this is Roger Senhouse, my young
friend from Oxford.

(PARTRIDGE *stretches down to shake hands with him as* LYTTON
continues his introductions.)

Ralph Partridge; and this is his friend Frances Marshall.
Oh, and this is Carrington.

(CARRINGTON *shakes hands with him, concealing whatever
affront she feels at* LYTTON*'s off-hand tone.*)

I'm sure there's a brush here for you somewhere.

ROGER: Oh, do you think so? I'm horribly bad at it.

LYTTON: Of course you are. Come, I'll show you the garden.

(LYTTON *smiles at him indulgently and shepherds him out into
the garden.*

    CARRINGTON *watches, through the window, slightly
concerned as* LYTTON *drapes a negligent arm around* ROGER*'s
shoulders and* ROGER *gently extracts a piece of food from*
LYTTON*'s beard.*

    She turns and crosses the room, noticing as she leaves how
PARTRIDGE, *up on the trestle, playfully ruffles* FRANCES*'s hair.*)

EXT. BACK GARDEN. DAY

Late afternoon. CARRINGTON *is sketching* LYTTON; *her pencil flies
across the paper.*

CARRINGTON: Good to be on our own again.

(LYTTON *looks out across the Downs, not answering for a
moment.*)

LYTTON: I must say I find these new young people wonderfully
refreshing. They have no morals and they never speak. It's
an enchanting combination. (*He looks across at her, then
continues in a low voice.*) I was standing outside a door,
trying to pluck up courage to knock, when suddenly it
swung open. I can scarcely believe it's happened.

CARRINGTON: I thought you were looking rather sprightly.

LYTTON: No, it's more than that; it was like being let into
paradise.

(CARRINGTON *looks up at* LYTTON, *alarmed.*)

INT. DRAWING-ROOM AT HAM SPRAY. EVENING

The room is half-decorated and still only provisionally furnished.
LYTTON *sits in the only armchair, watching, as a quarrel rages between* CARRINGTON *and* PARTRIDGE.

CARRINGTON: You wait until Lytton virtually bankrupts himself and then you announce you're not going to live here.

PARTRIDGE: I didn't say that. I said my life would have to be in London with Frances.

CARRINGTON: Why didn't you tell us this before?

PARTRIDGE: It's only just happened, I told you, we've only just decided.

CARRINGTON: How can you be so thoughtless? It's just not fair on Lytton.

(She looks at LYTTON, *as if in appeal; but he says nothing and she turns back to* PARTRIDGE *in exasperation. Close on* LYTTON, *as he watches.)*

It's not fair on any of us: to put our future in the hands of an outsider.

INT. ORIENTAL CLUB, LONDON. DAY

FRANCES MARSHALL *makes her way across the cavernous reaches of the Oriental Club, startling various aged members as they doze or thumb absently through newspapers. She arrives in front of* LYTTON, *installed in a colossal leather armchair. He looks up at her.*

LYTTON: How kind of you to come. I thought, of the four of us, you and I were the ones most likely to be able to discuss this sensibly. Do sit down.

(She does so, smiling politely, nervous but unintimidated.)

The fact of the matter is, if you and Ralph do plan to set up permanently in London, then I shall be forced to resell Ham Spray.

FRANCES: I understand.

LYTTON: You see, Ralph has become quite indispensable to us. We rely upon him for every practical decision.

FRANCES: Well, I certainly have no intention of . . . stopping Ralph from . . . seeing Carrington or interfering in any way. It's just that we're . . .

LYTTON: I know.

FRANCES: Ralph told me, when they first got married, they used to live in London during the week and . . .

LYTTON: Yes. It's a question of making a quite formal arrangement.

FRANCES: Couldn't we do the same, come down every weekend? I mean, the last thing I want to do . . .

(LYTTON *smiles, hugely relieved.*)

LYTTON: I knew you were the right person to talk to. Can I get you some tea?

EXT. DECK OF THE TRAWLER *SANS PAREIL*. DAY

At sea. CARRINGTON *grapples with the wheel, watched by a young man of twenty-six,* BERNARD (BEACUS) PENROSE. *He stands with his hands on his hips, blond, handsome, his face burnt brick red by sun and wind.*

CARRINGTON: (*Voiceover*) He likes to be called Beacus. He's not in the least curious, in fact rather remote, in other words, just what I need: and so beautiful. Lytton, the brass buckle on his belt.

INT. CABIN OF THE *SANS PAREIL*. DAY

PENROSE *is stretched out on one of the bunks.* CARRINGTON, *dressed, moves about the cabin making breakfast. As she passes, he reaches out and grabs hold of her skirt. She smiles and ruffles his hair. He takes her hand, quite roughly, and puts it to his lips. Then he puts two of her fingers in his mouth and nibbles at them. With his other hand, he lifts her skirt. She's wearing white stockings.*

PENROSE: Why don't you wear black stockings or dark brown? They show off a leg so much better than these things. And suspenders I like. Why don't you wear suspenders? (*His hand roams around under her skirt.*)

INT. HALLWAY AT HAM SPRAY. DAY

CARRINGTON *crosses the hallway to answer the phone.*

CARRINGTON: Hello?

INT. ORIENTAL CLUB. DAY

LYTTON *stands in the panelled alcove which contains the club's telephone.* SENHOUSE *sits on a nearby sofa, reading.*

LYTTON: Hello, it's me . . .

INT. HALLWAY. DAY
CARRINGTON *stands, holding the receiver, listening.*
LYTTON: I shan't be able to get back this evening.
CARRINGTON: Oh?

INT. ORIENTAL CLUB. DAY
LYTTON *is looking directly at* SENHOUSE.
LYTTON: As a matter of fact, I've done something rather
   impulsive . . .
   (SENHOUSE *looks up, catches* LYTTON*'s eye and smiles.*)

INT. HALLWAY. DAY
Close on CARRINGTON, *as* LYTTON *continues to speak. Her face
gradually disintegrates into a mask of suffering.*
LYTTON: (*Voiceover*) . . . I've taken some rooms in Gordon
   Square. It won't make the slightest difference to our
   arrangements, don't worry: it's just a way of circumventing
   these impossible difficulties, means I shan't have to keep
   depending on friends, taking hotel rooms, skulking about.
CARRINGTON: Sounds a very good idea. (*She hangs up.*)

INT. ORIENTAL CLUB. DAY
LYTTON *frowns, shrugs and hangs up. Then, his expression emphatic, he fetches something from his waistcoat pocket and bears down on* SENHOUSE. *With a flourish, he produces a key.* SENHOUSE *frowns at him interrogatively.*
LYTTON: Your key.
(SENHOUSE *hesitates.*)
SENHOUSE: Oh, no, Lytton, you know me. I'd only lose it. You keep it.
(*He smiles charmingly at* LYTTON, *who puts the key back in his pocket, clearly disturbed, and turns back to his book.*)

EXT. FALMOUTH HARBOUR. DAY
The Sans Pareil *rides at anchor in the harbour.*

INT. CABIN OF THE *SANS PAREIL*. DAY
The camera slowly approaches to find CARRINGTON *leaning forward across the bunk as* PENROSE *makes love to her, violently.*

EXT. GARDEN AT HAM SPRAY. DAY
Long shot through the gap in the laurel hedge. CARRINGTON *spurs on her horse and gallops through the pouring rain towards the back of the house.*

INT. HALLWAY. DAY
As CARRINGTON *emerges into the hall, drenched to the skin,* LYTTON *comes out of the drawing room to intercept her.*
LYTTON: What can you be thinking of, going out in this weather?
CARRINGTON: There's a reason for it, Lytton.
LYTTON: What? What can it possibly be?
CARRINGTON: *Je suis perdue.*
(*In the ensuing long silence, she sets off across the hallway and starts up the stairs. It's* LYTTON's *voice, full of sympathy, which stops her.*)
LYTTON: Are you sure?
(CARRINGTON *nods.*)
And you're sure you don't want it?
CARRINGTON: Oh, Lytton, I could never have a child. (*She turns*

and carries on up the stairs, adding in an undertone.) Unless it
was yours.
     (LYTTON *decides to ignore this, speaks again as she reaches the
     top of the stairs.*)
LYTTON: Have you told Beacus?
CARRINGTON: It's no good telling him, it'd only make him angry.
     I don't know why he puts up with me as it is.
LYTTON: I don't know why you put up with him.
CARRINGTON: Because he's the most exciting man I've ever slept
     with. And because I'm getting old.
     (*She starts moving along the landing towards her room;*
     LYTTON *speaks to her, stopping her in her tracks.*)
LYTTON: Now you know what it feels like.
     (*She looks down at him from the gallery.*)
CARRINGTON: I always did.
     (LYTTON *watches as she disappears down the corridor.*)

INT. DRAWING-ROOM AT HAM SPRAY. DAY
CARRINGTON *sits in front of an untouched cup of coffee, shivering,
grey-faced.* LYTTON *walks into the room with a piece of paper, which
he puts down on the table in front of her. He speaks very decisively.*
LYTTON: Here's the address of a very good man in London.

INT. CARRINGTON'S BEDROOM AT HAM SPRAY. DAY
CARRINGTON *is in bed.* LYTTON *advances into the room with a tray
of lunch.*
LYTTON: Well, this makes a change.
CARRINGTON: A very different pair of boots.
LYTTON: How are you feeling?
CARRINGTON: Rotten.
     (*He hands her the tray. She takes it, looking up at him.*)
     I know you don't like him, Lytton, or approve of him.
LYTTON: It's not that.
CARRINGTON: I'm sure he's as dim as a blind owl in a holly tree,
     but he never says anything, so you can't really tell.
     (*She's beginning to cry.* LYTTON *backs away and leaves the
     room.*)

66

EXT. GARDEN OF HAM SPRAY. NIGHT

A tracking shot, as before, passes through the opening in the laurel hedge.

    It stops at CARRINGTON *and* LYTTON *who are standing by the tree stump in the middle of the lawn. Through the lighted window of the games room* PENROSE *and* SENHOUSE *can be seen, playing table tennis. Distant clack of the ball. Next door, in the dining room,* PARTRIDGE *and* FRANCES *are moving around, clearing up.* LYTTON *sighs.*

LYTTON: D'you suppose they're going to play that wretched game all night?
    (*He sets off without waiting for an answer, goes into the house, passes through the games room in a meaningful way and out. Presently, the light goes on in the drawing room and he appears in the window, holding a newspaper, which he scarcely seems to be reading.*
    All this from CARRINGTON's *POV: now she decides to sit on the tree stump and watch.*
    The light goes out in the dining-room; PENROSE *and* SENHOUSE *finish playing;* SENHOUSE *goes to join* LYTTON *in the drawing room for a moment; the light goes on upstairs in* PARTRIDGE's *bedroom and he and* FRANCES *appear; then* PENROSE *appears in the next bedroom, pulling off his shirt as he crosses to the window; the light goes out in the drawing room.*
    Now, the camera slowly rises until it's at the level of the first floor: the light goes on in LYTTON's *bedroom and* SENHOUSE *appears in the window;* FRANCES *pulls the thin curtains, so that only her and* PARTRIDGE's *silhouettes can be seen as they move around the room and eventually embrace;* PENROSE *continues to undress;* LYTTON *comes up to* SENHOUSE *and stands with him in the window;* PENROSE *reappears in his window, still bare-chested, wearing blue-striped pyjama bottoms;* LYTTON *and* SENHOUSE *embrace.*
    The camera draws back to look at CARRINGTON, *isolated, unhappily watching, motionless on the tree stump.*)

SIX
LYTTON 1931–1932

INT. LYTTON'S STUDY AT HAM SPRAY. EVENING
LYTTON*'s study is a kind of comfortable upstairs library with a large
desk. A portrait of Voltaire dominates the room, which at the
moment is in darkness.* LYTTON *sits at his desk, his face buried in his
hands. The door opens, throwing a shaft of light into the room and*
CARRINGTON *appears. She's immediately aware that something is the
matter and hurries over to* LYTTON.
CARRINGTON: What's the matter?
   (LYTTON *looks up at her: his face is streaked with tears. He's
   holding a letter.*)
LYTTON: I've had a letter from Roger. He's not coming down
   next week. He says I've let him mean too much to me. He
   says I've oppressed him.
   (CARRINGTON *puts her arms around him, struggling with her
   own pain.*)
   He's right, of course. One doesn't intend to let it get out of
   hand; and then it does; and then there's this blackness.
   (*He begins to sob uncontrollably.* CARRINGTON *draws him to her
   and strokes his hair.*)

EXT. DECK OF THE SANS PAREIL. DAY
CARRINGTON *is steering the boat and* PENROSE *is winching in a sail.*
CARRINGTON: Sometimes . . . (*She breaks off, but then can't
   prevent herself from saying it.*) Sometimes I think you don't
   like me very much.
   (PENROSE *looks at her, expressionless.*)
PENROSE: No, no. It's not that. I'm devoted to you, you know
   that. It's just . . .
CARRINGTON: Go on.
PENROSE: It's just you don't really attract me sexually. To be
   honest.
   (CARRINGTON *stares at him, horrified, the blood drained from
   her face.*)

INT. DRAWING-ROOM AT HAM SPRAY. DAY
LYTTON *sits in the window, being painted by* CARRINGTON.
LYTTON: That man from the London Group, who keeps offering
   you an exhibition: why don't you take him up on it?
CARRINGTON: I've told you before, I don't want an exhibition.
   That isn't why I do it. I paint when I feel well and it makes
   me feel even better. I'm not interested in selling them.
   They're for us.
   (*Silence.*)
LYTTON: So, you're all right now?
CARRINGTON: Yes, I am. At least it's been a great mercy, not
   being in the wrong this time.
LYTTON: I've been thinking of giving you a little pension, just a
   hundred a year or so.
CARRINGTON: Do keep still, you're causing havoc.

EXT./INT. DINING-ROOM AT HAM SPRAY. EVENING
Seen through the window, LYTTON *and* CARRINGTON *eat their dinner
and drink their wine, bathed in a pool of gentle light.*

EXT. GARDEN OF HAM SPRAY. DAY
LYTTON *sits in his deck-chair, reading to* CARRINGTON, *his voice
unheard.*

INT. LYTTON'S STUDY. DAY
LYTTON *and* CARRINGTON *have been having tea. Now,*
CARRINGTON *makes a move to clear away.*
CARRINGTON: I'd better leave you to get on.
LYTTON: Oh, God, no, please stay for a while. (*He sighs
   theatrically.*) I have heard rumours to the effect that there
   are people who actually enjoy writing. Can this be true? I
   loathe it. All that work and then at the end of it some slim
   volume, what's the point, I ask myself.
CARRINGTON: Think of posterity.
LYTTON: Why? What's posterity ever done for me?
   (*They smile.* LYTTON *reflects for a moment.*)
   I've done my best to keep it quiet, but I'm an ambitious
   man. I thought if I could cut through all that atrocious fog
   of superstition that poisons so many people's lives, I might

70

be able to do some good in the world. But the truth is, I've always been better at living than I ever was at writing.

CARRINGTON: What's wrong with that? (*She looks at him for a moment.*) I don't think you have any idea how happy you've made me.

EXT. GARDEN OF HAM SPRAY. EVENING
CARRINGTON, PARTRIDGE, FRANCES, *and three or four other young* GUESTS *are listening to* LYTTON *in full spate. Drinks have been served and the sun is setting over the Downs.*

LYTTON: Anyway, I was about to speak to this black-haired tart in gumboots, when I suddenly noticed a much prettier tart, blond, in the gallery next door. So I abandoned the gumboots and began to sidle up to the blond, very fetching he was, pink and chubby. I was about to murmur something seductive into his delicious ear when suddenly the light fell on him and I realized who he was. (*He leans forward, stage whisper.*) The Prince of Wales!
(*General laughter. Then, completely unexpectedly,* LYTTON *vomits.* CARRINGTON *hurries over to him, concerned and begins mopping up.*)
Oh, my God, I'm most terribly sorry.

INT. DINING-ROOM AT HAM SPRAY. DAY
CARRINGTON *and* PARTRIDGE *sit at the kitchen table.* PARTRIDGE *is staring morosely at a piece of untouched toast and marmalade.* CARRINGTON *speaks with a strange brittle cheerfulness.*

CARRINGTON: Oh, come on, Ralph, don't be so gloomy. There's nothing to worry about.
(PARTRIDGE *looks up at her, startled.*)

INT. LYTTON'S BEDROOM AT HAM SPRAY. EVENING
LYTTON's *bedroom is magnificently appointed, notably with a gold Boris Anrep mosaic of a reclining hermaphrodite over the fireplace and Giotto angels on a wall painted Giotto blue by* CARRINGTON.
A uniformed NURSE, *grey-haired, bespectacled and forbidding, sits near the window, knitting in the half-light.* CARRINGTON *pours cologne on to a damp handkerchief and dabs it on* LYTTON's *forehead. He smiles feebly at her.*

71

INT. DINING-ROOM AT HAM SPRAY. EVENING
CARRINGTON, BRENAN *and* PARTRIDGE *are sitting in silence sipping soup. At the head of the table is* LYTTON'*s empty chair.* CARRINGTON *raises her spoon towards her mouth, but can't quite bring herself to eat.*

INT. LYTTON'S BEDROOM AT HAM SPRAY. EVENING
CARRINGTON *comes into* LYTTON'*s dark bedroom, leading* BRENAN *by the hand.* PARTRIDGE *brings up the rear. They stand by* LYTTON'*s bedside. He's looking perceptibly thinner and weaker. He smiles at them.*
LYTTON: Well, my dears, shall we go to Malaga in the spring?

EXT. HAM SPRAY HOUSE. DAY
The camera tracks through the laurel hedge. The lawns are white with frost. Cloudless sky.

INT. LYTTON'S BEDROOM AT HAM SPRAY. DAY
LYTTON *lies in bed. He opens his eyes and looks over at* CARRINGTON, *who is standing, looking out of the window.*
LYTTON: Carrington. Where's Carrington?
   (CARRINGTON *turns, surprised.*)
CARRINGTON: I'm here.
LYTTON: Why isn't she here? I want her.
   (CARRINGTON *hurries to the bedside and takes his hand.*)
CARRINGTON: Here I am.
LYTTON: Where is she? I love her. I always wanted to marry
   Carrington and I never did.
   (*He sinks back, exhausted.* CARRINGTON *stands holding his hand for a long moment.*
      The door opens. The NURSE *comes in.* CARRINGTON *lets go of* LYTTON'*s hand and hurries across to her, speaks in an urgent whisper.*)
CARRINGTON: Is there any chance he'll live?
   (*The* NURSE *looks at her, momentarily surprised. Then she answers, not unkindly.*)
NURSE: Oh, no, I don't think so. Not now.

EXT. COURTYARD OF HAM SPRAY. NIGHT
Moonlight. CARRINGTON *creeps out of the back door and across the courtyard, her breath rising in the cold night air. She passes the stable door, where Belle's white head is visible and presses on to the garage door. At first she can't get it open. She tugs at it with increasing desperation.*

INT. LYTTON'S BEDROOM AT HAM SPRAY. NIGHT
LYTTON *suddenly jerks convulsively and gasps for breath.* PARTRIDGE, *who's been sitting with him, is on his feet immediately and the* NURSE, *who has been dozing, comes to. She hurries over to* LYTTON. PARTRIDGE *stands a second, then leaves the room, moving quickly.*

INT. UPSTAIRS CORRIDOR AT HAM SPRAY. NIGHT
PARTRIDGE *runs along the corridor, opens the door of* CARRINGTON'S *bedroom.*

INT. CARRINGTON'S BEDROOM AT HAM SPRAY. NIGHT
PARTRIDGE *switches the light on.* CARRINGTON'S *room is empty.* PARTRIDGE *frowns, puzzled. Then a terrible thought strikes him.*

EXT. COURTYARD OF HAM SPRAY. NIGHT
PARTRIDGE *dashes across the courtyard, grapples desperately with the garage door and wrenches it open.*

INT. GARAGE. NIGHT
The interior of the car, a green 1928 Sunbeam, is an island of light. PARTRIDGE, *coughing and spluttering, rushes to the car door, opens it, reaches in and turns off the ignition. Then he leans across the back seat, grabs hold of* CARRINGTON *and tugs at her body. She's unconscious. He struggles to get her out of the car, tears streaming down his face.*

INT. CARRINGTON'S BEDROOM AT HAM SPRAY. DAY
CARRINGTON *grapples fiercely with* PARTRIDGE, *who's holding her down on the bed, so that the doctor,* DR STARKEY SMITH, *who's hovering in the background, can administer an injection.* CARRINGTON *is screaming at them.*

73

CARRINGTON: No! No! Go away! Go away!

STARKEY SMITH: Now, Mrs Partridge . . .

CARRINGTON: Go away!

(*He succeeds in giving the injection.* CARRINGTON *goes limp and* PARTRIDGE *gathers her up in his arms and kisses her feverishly. He looks shattered.*)

PARTRIDGE: How could you do it?

INT. LYTTON'S BEDROOM AT HAM SPRAY. DAY

CARRINGTON, *deathly pale and unsteady on her feet,* PARTRIDGE *and the* NURSE, *stand in a semi-circle at the foot of the bed.*

After a while, LYTTON *speaks, scarcely more than a whisper, but clearly audible.*

LYTTON: If this is dying, then I don't think much of it. (*Hint of a smile. He is so pale as to be almost transparent.*)

(PARTRIDGE's *face is contorted with an almost unbearable strain.* CARRINGTON *looks greenish, desperate.*

They wait. Gradually, LYTTON *stops breathing. Long silence. Then the* NURSE *steps forward, puts her hand on his heart, waits and shakes her head. She moves away. The others stand in shocked silence. Then,* CARRINGTON *moves forward. She touches* LYTTON's *forehead, then recoils, drawing her hand away involuntarily.*)

CARRINGTON: You're so cold.

(PARTRIDGE *lowers his head.*)

FADE

INT. SITTING-ROOM OF GERTLER'S FLAT AT 22 KEMPLAY ROAD. DAY

GERTLER, *now forty, still youthful, but with the watchful expression of a man long used to suffering, is opening a parcel. With him is his wife,* MARJORIE, *a rather beautiful woman of thirty.*

GERTLER: It's a wedding present. From Carrington.

(*He's unwrapped three plates of her design.* MARJORIE *smiles.*)

MARJORIE: Only two years late, do you suppose that's a record?

(*But* GERTLER *is disturbed. He turns over one of the plates, considering.*)

GERTLER: Strange.

EXT. TERRACE AT GARSINGTON. DAY

OTTOLINE, *fifty-eight now, battered but still grandiose, a chiffon scarf wound around her neck, her make-up as strikingly erratic as ever, is sorting through her morning mail. One letter in particular strikes her attention. She opens it and a number of sepia photographs spill out on the table.*

CARRINGTON: (*Voiceover*) Dear Ottoline, It is to you I owe the happiness, probably, of my life with Lytton. I thank you for those days at Garsington when I grew to love him. Yours, Carrington.

(OTTOLINE *stops looking through the photographs, lays them aside and looks away, moved.*)

EXT. GARDEN OF HAM SPRAY. DAY

CARRINGTON *is planting bulbs under the trees.*

INT. DRAWING-ROOM AT HAM SPRAY. DAY

PARTRIDGE *stands at the window, looking anxiously out at* CARRINGTON. FRANCES *joins him.*

FRANCES: What's she doing?

PARTRIDGE: Planting bulbs.

FRANCES: Well, that's surely a good sign, isn't it?

PARTRIDGE: Yes. Yes, it is.

INT./EXT. DINING-ROOM AT HAM SPRAY. DAY

CARRINGTON *stands at the window; behind her* PARTRIDGE *and* FRANCES *eat lunch in silence.*

  CARRINGTON*'s POV: a couple of rabbits are jumping about on the lawn.*

EXT. FRONT DRIVE OF HAM SPRAY. DAY

CARRINGTON *drives the Sunbeam up to the front of the house and pulls up.*

  PARTRIDGE *can be seen at the window, on the telephone. Now, he replaces the receiver and comes hurrying out of the house.*

  CARRINGTON *gets out of the car, awkwardly. She's carrying a double-barrelled shot gun.* PARTRIDGE *intercepts her and she straightens up to face him, her expression defiant.*

PARTRIDGE: What the hell are you doing with that?

CARRINGTON: I borrowed it from Bryan. It's for the rabbits.
PARTRIDGE: Now, look here . . .
    (CARRINGTON *disappears into the house, calling back to him.*)
CARRINGTON: It's for the rabbits!

INT. DRAWING-ROOM AT HAM SPRAY. EVENING
CARRINGTON *and* PARTRIDGE. *He looks ragged with exhaustion: she, calm, almost serene.*
CARRINGTON: Look Ralph, it's no good going on like this.
PARTRIDGE: I can't leave you!
CARRINGTON: You know perfectly well I'm going to France next
    week, it's all arranged, the tickets are bought . . .
PARTRIDGE: Yes, I know . . .
CARRINGTON: And now, I want to be on my own for a bit, that's
    all. I can't stand the strain of worrying about you worrying
    about me.
PARTRIDGE: Listen . . .
CARRINGTON: I must be on my own.

EXT. FRONT DRIVE OF HAM SPRAY HOUSE. DAY
CARRINGTON *kisses* FRANCES, *who gets into the passenger seat of the Sunbeam. Then,* CARRINGTON *and* PARTRIDGE *stand for a moment looking at each other.*
CARRINGTON: Don't worry. I'll be all right.
PARTRIDGE: Yes.
    (*He puts his arms round her and she lets him kiss her. Then, just as he's about to break away, she kisses him quite fiercely.*)
CARRINGTON: I want you to be very happy.
    (*She lets him go. He stands there a moment, shocked by the implications of what she's just said, his face racked by contradictory emotions.*
        Then, abruptly, he breaks away, gets into the car, starts it up and drives away. FRANCES *waves;* PARTRIDGE *doesn't look back.*
        CARRINGTON *stands, a hand raised in farewell, caught in suddenly emerging sunlight, beatific. On sound, the Schubert Quintet.*)

EXT. COURTYARD OF HAM SPRAY. DAY
A ferocious clatter, as CARRINGTON *empties her tubes of paint and brushes into the metal dustbin.*

EXT. GARDEN OF HAM SPRAY. DAY
CARRINGTON *stands by a blazing bonfire, a pile of* LYTTON*'s old clothes beside her which she feeds one by one into the fire. Finally, glinting at the bottom of the pile, are his spectacles. She picks them up, holds them for the briefest moment and then throws them in the fire. The frames curl and buckle in the heat.*
CARRINGTON: (*Voiceover*) No one will ever know the utter
    happiness of our life together.

INT. DRAWING-ROOM AT HAM SPRAY. EVENING
CARRINGTON *is lying motionless on the sofa. Draped across her body is one of Lytton's tweed jackets and spread out on her face, covering it, is one of his initialled handkerchiefs.*
CARRINGTON: (*Voiceover*) It is impossible to think that every day
    of my life you will be away.

INT. LYTTON'S STUDY. EVENING
Pan slowly round the bookshelves and along one shelf of Lytton's books, all beautifully bound in a uniform edition. Finally the camera

77

reaches CARRINGTON. *She is sitting on the floor in a corner of the darkening room arms wrapped round her knees, holding* LYTTON*'s binoculars, staring into space, eyes dead.*

CARRINGTON: (*Voiceover*) I write in an empty book. I cry in an empty room.

INT. LYTTON'S BEDROOM AT HAM SPRAY. NIGHT
CARRINGTON *opens Lytton's wardrobe. It's now empty except for his purple silk dressing gown. She slips it off the hanger and strokes her cheek against it.*

CARRINGTON: Oh, my very darling Lytton.

INT. CARRINGTON'S BEDROOM AT HAM SPRAY. DAWN
CARRINGTON *wakes. It's still almost dark. The purple dressing gown is lying across the foot of the bed. She gets out of bed and puts the dressing gown on.*

INT. DINING-ROOM AT HAM SPRAY. DAWN
CARRINGTON *has eaten an apple.*

She puts down The Times *for March 11th next to two or three opened letters, neatly stacked. She takes a sip from a half-empty mug of tea, puts it down and rises, calm and decisive, to her feet. She leaves the room.*

INT. HALLWAY AND STAIRCASE. DAWN
The camera follows CARRINGTON *across the hallway, up the stairs and back along the upstairs landing.*

INT. CARRINGTON'S BEDROOM. DAWN
CARRINGTON *walks into the room, moves to the wardrobe, reaches in and brings out the shotgun.*

She pushes the wardrobe shut and crosses to the cheval mirror, standing on BRENAN*'s rug.*

She puts the butt of the gun against the floor, tucks the barrel in under her heart and checks her position in the mirror.

Then, she leans forward, closes her eyes and pulls the trigger. Nothing.

She opens her eyes and lifts the gun. A moment, before she realizes. She has forgotten to release the safety-catch.

She does so, puts the gun back in position.

Long silence. She looks in the mirror. She smiles. She closes her eyes and slowly bows forward over the shotgun.

EXT. HAM SPRAY HOUSE. DAWN

The camera tracks through the doorway in the laurel hedge and stops, as the second movement of the Schubert Quintet comes to an end.

The house. Five seconds.

Explosion. Darkness.